eve day spiritual habits

SMALL, SIMPLE WAYS TO
TRANSFORM YOUR FAITH,
STARTING NOW

HANNA SEYMOUR

ebury
vine

EBURY VINE

UK | USA | Canada | Ireland | Australia
India | New Zealand | South Africa

Ebury Vine is part of the Penguin Random House group of companies
whose addresses can be found at global.penguinrandomhouse.com

Penguin Random House UK
One Embassy Gardens, 8 Viaduct Gardens, London SW11 7BW

penguin.co.uk

Penguin
Random House
UK

First published in the United States by Worthy Books, a division
of Hachette Book Group, Inc. in 2026
First published in Great Britain by Ebury Vine in 2026
Copyright © Hanna Seymour 2026
The moral right of the author has been asserted.

No part of this book may be used or reproduced in any manner for the purpose of training artificial
intelligence technologies or systems. This work is reserved from text and data mining (Article 4(3)
Directive (EU) 2019/790).

Typeset by Six Red Marbles UK, Thetford, Norfolk

Printed and bound in Great Britain by Clays Ltd, Elcograf S.p.A.

The authorised representative in the EEA is Penguin Random House Ireland,
Morrison Chambers, 32 Nassau Street, Dublin D02 YH68

A CIP catalogue record for this book is available from the British Library

ISBN 9781911764045

CONTENTS

DEDICATED TO
ALL THE WEARY ONES

A PRAYER FOR THIS BOOK, AND YOU, DEAR READER:

Lord of all heaven and earth, people and books,
May Your Spirit fill the words these pages hold.
May You give insight and wisdom to the reader.
Counteract anything written that is wrong.
Let only Your truth find entrance into their hearts and minds.
To those who hold this book in their hands, speak to them, as
*   only You can.*
Take my feeble attempt to encourage and equip your beloved
*   children.*
Radically open their eyes to Your invitation of an everyday,
*   extraordinary life with You.*
Fill my words with Your resurrection power in their minds
*   and souls.*
That they may know You more intimately, love You more
*   deeply, and experience a greater fellowship with You all*
*   the days of their lives.*

INTRODUCTION

It should go without saying that I believe in the content of this book down to the marrow in my bones. I believe that we can all live our ordinary days of changing diapers, taking work calls, planning meals, cleaning kitchens, arguing with burgeoning lawyers (a.k.a. toddlers or teens), balancing the budget, juggling childcare, walking the dog, scrubbing crayon off the wall, sweating at the gym, handling difficult coworkers, managing school drop-offs and pick-ups, folding laundry, and more (phew! How can we do even more?!) while in constant connection with our Creator. We can experience spiritual growth amidst the circus we call living, and our ordinary days can truly add up to an extraordinary life.

And yet, I do not for one second wish you to think I'm somehow an expert in all of this. Just like you, I lose my temper with my kids. I get frustrated with my husband. I get tired of all the laundry, cleaning, meal prep, and booty wiping. I have hopes and dreams that I often surrender back to God out of fear that they're selfish rather than holy. I do not spend hours a day studying scripture or on my knees in prayer.

Frankly, I would love to do that, but I am not a monk or a nun. Instead, God gave me a husband, three children, a few part-time jobs, and several other plates to spin. This is the life He has given me, and so this is the life He expects me to commune with Him. He planted me here in this soil. Just as He has planted you in your own unique soil or situation. And make no mistake, He has cultivated and tilled the soil for the exact purpose of growing us into flourishing, fruit-bearing trees.

You may have heard the saying "Never trust a leader without a limp."[1] To be honest, there are days when I'm not sure I'm even standing upright enough to walk with a limp. I'm merely crawling. But the longer I walk or crawl with Christ, the more convinced I am that it's not about being strong, independent, or seemingly having it all together. More than anything, God wants us to be totally and utterly dependent on Him. It's in our weakness, our vulnerability, that He draws us to Him.

So, if I may, I'd like to offer you the most vulnerable version of myself. I'm not perfect, and I'm no expert, but if you want a friend to crawl with you shoulder to shoulder through the trenches of life and talk about Jesus along the way, I'm your girl. And the best part is: God goes with us. When we bring awareness to His presence, when we lean on Him for strength, when we ask Him which way to turn next, we transform more and more into who He created us to be—a reflection of His very self.

Finding Spiritual Growth While Serving as a Wife, Mom, Podcast Producer, Nonprofit Administrator, Maid, Chef, Personal Assistant, Chauffeur, Prison Guard, and FBI Negotiator

This story begins with a three-and-a-half-year-old, a two-year-old, and an infant. Yes, I'm tired just thinking about it. God gave me three babies in three and a half years, and I wouldn't recommend it, but here we are. Still standing (or crawling, as we've already discussed).*

On this particular day, I had scheduled a photographer to meet us in our neighborhood for a thirty-minute session during which I expected to capture a still image of our newly minted family of five that could be slapped on a Christmas card and mailed to our two hundred closest friends.**

I had meticulously planned our color-coordinated outfits days prior to this momentous occasion, but as any mom reading this will antici-pate, no one wanted to wear the aforementioned outfits. As I combed and styled hair, there was weeping and gnashing of teeth. Even more tears gushed as my two-year-old argued, pleaded, and yelled that the shoes I was using my mama-bear, brute strength to cram his feet into were too small. There was screaming while the almost-always-happy baby would not be consoled with bottle, breast, or pacifier. Apparently she was in cahoots with her brothers and did not like her outfit, found it scratchy, needed tags cut out, or simply did not want to wear that shade of blue. Perhaps they had a meeting the night before and agreed in soli-darity to take me down that morning.

Yet, I prevailed. *Don't you dare come between a mom and her Christ-mas card.* Despite the chaos and emotional scarring that certainly took place, everyone was locked and loaded in our brand-new minivan, and we were finally set to pull out of the garage only a few minutes later

---

* This feels like a good time to introduce my use of footnotes. There are many times throughout this book when I have more to say, but I'm aware that I'm including far too much detail for some readers. So, the footnotes will be here for those of you who want all—and I mean ALL—of my thoughts. But for those of you who don't have time or can't be bothered, feel free to just skip right over them.

** Can we just pause here for a minute and talk about the insanity that is Christmas cards? I know some of y'all love them. According to you, Gary Chapman got the five love languages wrong because there are actually six, and the sixth is obviously Christmas cards. But y'all, why are we spending hundreds of dollars to mail a photo of our family to hundreds of our "closest" friends—many of whom we haven't spoken to in over a year?! I just don't get it. But I digress . . .

than planned. Hallelujah! I envisioned the angels were applauding me from heaven, high-fiving one another for the assistance they no doubt gave.

The garage door opened, the van began to back out, and CRUNCH.

I won't say who was driving the brand-new minivan (but it wasn't me), and I definitely won't mention the fact that they forgot to close the passenger sliding door. But when he (I mean—the anonymous driver) began to pull out of the garage, the brand-new minivan door and our garage door frame had a collision, and the minivan lost. And while I won't go into detail, our brand-new—*did I mention it was brand-new?!*—minivan now had a brand-new, two-foot-wide gap where the door should have been.*

I yelled words that were not praiseworthy.

As I write this years later, I can chuckle at the memory, but in the moment, I was absolutely not laughing. Amidst the anger and exhaustion, I remember thinking, *This is the perfect illustration of what this entire season of life feels like.* It's chaos; there are too many moving parts, tears, accidents, and occasional expletives. There are such big feelings—of course from my kids, but also from me. I am spinning my wheels, trying so hard, yet I keep dropping plates that shatter on the floor. I'm tired, depleted, and busier than I want to be—but I can't see a way to simplify things more. Change fewer diapers? Do less laundry? Feed the hangry people only two times a day?** Everything is necessary.

I mean no disrespect to the Apostle Paul, who was thrown into

---

* In total transparency, I need to tell you that my husband read this section and felt it vital I include the information that all three children were screaming bloody murder, hence why he did not realize the door was open (because he should have heard the beeps alerting him) and how what came to be, well, came to be. Also, whoops, didn't mean to out him. Just pretend you didn't read this!

** Heck, just three times would be great. Why do they always want snacks?!

prison, beaten, and shipwrecked multiple times, but when I read his words "We are hard pressed on every side, but not crushed; perplexed, but not in despair; persecuted, but not abandoned; struck down, but not destroyed,"* I think, *Same, brother.*

And it's not just me. These are the exact same sentiments I heard from more than two thousand women in a survey I conducted while in seminary. A majority—66 percent—said they often feel exhausted (physically, spiritually, emotionally, and/or mentally). The most common response to "What three words best describe this season of your life?" was *busy* or *full* (reported 793 times) and then *challenging, hard, stressful, overwhelming,* or *chaotic* (written 473 times).

But busy, challenging, hard, or even chaotic isn't all bad. We have dreamed, prayed, and even begged God for a lot—if not all—of the things that we're juggling: careers, marriages, kids, friendships, ministries, hobbies. While the majority of women said they were exhausted, the majority—another 66 percent—also said they were content with their lives.

So, we may be juggling a lot of things and living at maximum capacity, but we're content because this is how we expect this season of life to be. It may be insane, but we're making it, gosh darn it.

Interestingly, 65 percent of respondents said they were not satisfied with their spiritual lives. They want to prioritize spiritual growth; they want more discipline in their spiritual lives (and let's face it, all other aspects of life), but when day-to-day life is so physically, emotionally, and mentally demanding, it's hard to create space for spiritual growth. We may want to read the Bible, cultivate habits of prayer, or be reflective and intentional to keep a spiritual mindset throughout our day, but how can we do anything more when we are already burning the candle at both ends?

* 2 Corinthians 4:8–9, NIV

Prior to having children, I was very consistent when it came to spiritual disciplines. I read my Bible daily, had prayer journals I worked through, memorized scripture, and taught and led Bible studies. But after I became a mom, I struggled. I was so tired. I had a baby who didn't sleep great and nursed throughout the night. I couldn't drag myself out of bed even one minute before he woke up. So I said adios to my morning Bible study time. Even as I sat in a rocking chair nursing him, my brain was too tired and foggy to even think about connecting with God. Overnight, I went from having multiple daily rhythms that encouraged spiritual growth and connection to God to having nothing. My routine was so rocked by this tiny new human that I began to flounder spiritually. It wasn't a crisis of faith, but I felt so distant from God. What once was a vital, vibrant foundation of my life had become an empty void.

Maybe it wasn't a new baby for you, but I bet you resonate with the feelings of being at or over capacity. You're exhausted; maybe you're drowning. It's not that you don't have a lot of wonderful things in your life—things that bring you deep joy—but you're still barely making it day to day. You prioritize the things that have to get done and put anything that seems like a luxury on the back burner. For women, I've noticed this often includes anything that pertains to our own health and wellness—working out, prioritizing good nutrition, sleeping well, pursuing friendships that feed our souls, and most importantly, practicing any kind of habits that foster our own spiritual growth.

We all know spiritual disciplines are important, but beyond some light Bible reading and occasional toss-up prayers, they only seem realistic for the professional Christian. When and how is a busy mom of three preschoolers, or a woman with a demanding career and personal life, supposed to carve out time for spiritual disciplines? When we're already feeling overwhelmed and maxed out, how can we possibly add more to our overflowing plates?

We need to reframe our perspective on spiritual disciplines to see them as spiritual habits, no longer viewed as lofty, time-consuming, backbreaking practices but as small, continual habits, fueled by God's Spirit. They aren't just another task on our to-do list, but rhythms we grow to crave—simple, daily habits that turn our ordinary days into extraordinary lives through constant fellowship with Jesus. The last fifteen years of research in the field of habit formation are going to help us immensely with this. We're going to look at how to create habits that really stick,* as well as how small habits compound over time to create major change, and we'll apply that knowledge to the practice of spiritual habits.

My intention for this book is to give you hope—hope that there is spiritual growth to be had amidst a chaotic life and a deep well of joy to be experienced by finding new rhythms and new ways to implement small, spiritual habits throughout your ordinary days. I want to remind you that it's not only possible to prioritize your spiritual health, it is actually vital to your day-to-day survival. Prioritizing your spiritual growth isn't a luxury, it's a necessity.

By looking at habit-formation science, providing a brief overview of common spiritual disciplines, and engaging in a realistic conversation about what that practically looks like for the everyday woman, I want to show you how you've been invited to walk step-by-step with the Creator of the Universe as you go throughout your day. By walking closely with Him, your run-of-the-mill and even chaotic days are fertile soil for producing a spiritually deep and rich life.

---

* No more SMART goals, no more outcome-based goals, no more "go big or go home" mentality.

Where We're Going

Look, you're busy. We've covered that. So, I'm not about to write a tome detailing every facet of behavioral science or a treatise on spiritual growth including every possible spiritual discipline we could be practicing.

In honor of your time, I have distilled the core elements of habit formation science down to one chapter. Chapter one will be an overview on spiritual growth and disciplines—what they are, what they're not, and why we need to change our perspective on them. Chapter two will be everything we need to radically reframe the way we think about creating new habits—particularly when it comes to spiritual habits. Then, the following six chapters will zero in on a handful of spiritual habits I believe will be most helpful to you in your current season of life: biblical intake, prayer, solitude, thanksgiving and celebration, meaningful friendship, and practicing the presence of God.

We'll get into this more at the end of chapter two, but after you've read chapters one and two, I want you to pick only one spiritual habit to focus on at first.

So, you may read the book in its entirety (and it's my sincerest hope that you do) to get a lay of the land, and then decide which spiritual habit you want to apply first. Or you may decide to jump straight to chapter five because you need solitude in your life like queso needs chips. Regardless, I want you to feel the freedom to go where you're most drawn, take your time, and start small.

Another idea that would make me happier than Ralphie getting his Red Ryder BB gun should you implement it: Grab a small group of women you enjoy and slowly read the book together. Meet once a month or every other week to discuss and implement one chapter at a time. Then just watch what God does!*

---

* For a free small-group discussion guide: hannaseymour.com/ESH.

But the bottom line when it comes to creating habits that last is that we have to start small, which means we'll choose one spiritual habit, create one to three very small habits (which I call Seed Habits), and slowly build from there. My hope is that you choose to come back to this book over and over through the years as you think about how to implement dozens more Seed Habits. You're going to see how these seemingly tiny habits cause major spiritual growth, and you're going to want to come back for more.

CHAPTER ONE

The Practice
of Spiritual Habits

"Your work is to rest in Me."

—Unattributed poem quoted in
Hudson Taylor's Spiritual Secret[1]

Visualize your favorite elderly woman. Maybe she's someone you personally know—your grandma, a neighbor, or a woman at your church. Maybe she's someone you know of, like Dolly Parton,* fashion icon Iris Apfel, or Maya Angelou. Maybe she's a character from television or film—Maggie Smith's Dowager Countess of Grantham in *Downton Abbey* or her Professor McGonagall in *Harry Potter*, or Grandma Annie in *The Proposal*, played by Betty White. Whoever she is, why is she your favorite? What draws you to her?

While I don't know who you picked, I wonder if she's anything like mine: She's confident—she knows exactly who she is and makes

---

* Sorry for calling you elderly, Dolly. Age is just a number!

11

no apologies for it. She's sharp. She is wise and strategic. She has plenty of opinions and knows when to keep them to herself (though she rarely does) and when to share them. She is playful. Despite her age, there is still an element of youthfulness to her. Whether it's a wink, a daredevil grin, or childlike joy, she refuses to become an old curmudgeon.* She has a steadfastness and peace about her. She's seen it all, heard the song, written the story, nothing surprises her, and she can still smile at the future. Maybe she's just the sweetest, happiest, kindest, most caring, generous person you've ever met.

Now visualize yourself at ninety years old. Who are you? How will you be described?

As Christians, as people who profess Jesus as Lord and raise our hands to say, "Yep, me! I want to follow Jesus! I want to love Him wholeheartedly and be His hands and feet in this world! I want my life to overflow with His love!" we should be the most joyful, peaceful, confident, compassionate, loving, generous people on the planet—especially by the age of ninety.

But if we're honest, most of us struggle with being all of those things now. We're tired, we're beaten, we're worn, we're scared, we're stressed. Life is hard and our world often feels hopeless.

Yet this is where the Apostle Paul's words give us hope. "Don't copy the behavior and customs of this world, but let God transform you into a new person by changing the way you think. Then you will learn to know God's will for you, which is good and pleasing and perfect" (Romans 12: 1–2). We have a choice. We can let the world conform us to its liking, *or* we can allow God to transform us into a new creation.**

---

* Even Maggie Smith's characters in *Downton Abbey* and *Harry Potter* had a bit of childlike spark to them.
** See also 2 Corinthians 5:17.

What sticks out to me about this verse is that it's one or the other. Either the world is molding me into its image (it's squeezing me, crushing me, taking what God intended and deforming it to make me unrecognizable from God's good creation, and instead blend in with everybody else on earth), or God is transforming me into a woman (into His good, redeemed, beautiful creation) that I can't become on my own strength or initiative. There's no in between. So, the question the Apostle Paul leads us to ask is: *Who or what is molding me?* Is it our world—the media, your culture, your friends—molding you into a person motivated by fear and anxiety? Shaping you into someone who views others as enemies? Turning you into a worshiper of power and money? Is it your dysfunctional family circumstances that taught you a distorted version of love or made you feel unwanted and unworthy? Is it loneliness? Cancer? Heartbreak? Or is Jesus Himself molding you?

Something or someone is molding you, and the answer to that question forecasts who you will be and what you will be like when you're ninety.

Jen Wilkin wrote, "We will not wake up ten years from now and find we have passively taken on the character of God."[2]

While it is the complete work of God's Spirit to transform us, we have a part to play in our own spiritual growth. We can't sit on the couch and binge-watch Netflix for hours each night and expect God to do His part. We have to choose, in faithful obedience, to submit to His Spirit in our lives.

Dallas Willard, who in many ways is the "father" of spiritual formation* in the twentieth and twenty-first century, said there are three

---

* Willard is now with Jesus, but if he heard me call him this, he'd likely try to "fade into the wall" (his words). But whether he likes it or not, most spiritual formation and discipline books quote him ad nauseam, and for good reason! (This book included!)

essential elements (what he termed "the golden triangle") to our individual spiritual growth: the practice of spiritual disciplines, the work of the Holy Spirit, and enduring trials and difficulties.[3] As Willard points out, we see all three of these elements in successive order in Paul's letter to the Philippian church:

> Therefore, my dear friends . . . continue to **work out your salvation** with fear and trembling, for it is **God who works in you** to will and to act in order to fulfill his good purpose. Do everything without grumbling or arguing, so that you may become blameless and pure, children of God without fault in a **warped and crooked generation**. Then you will shine among them like stars in the sky as you hold firmly to the word of life (Philippians 2:12–16a, NIV).

When Paul speaks of "working out your salvation," he is not suggesting that Christ's death and resurrection weren't enough. In fact, Paul makes it clear multiple times throughout his writings that it is by faith in Jesus alone that we are saved, not by anything we can do on our own merit.* Christ's blood cleansed us from our sin problem,** yet we still sin. While He removed our guilt and shame and made us right before God,*** He is also always at work slowly, caringly uprooting all kinds of sin in our hearts and minds and transforming us moment by moment to look more like Him.

So, we "work out our salvation" with deep reverence by continually choosing God's way and not ours, by continually dying to self,

---

* See Ephesians 2:5–8, 8–9; Acts 15:11; Romans 3:24, 5:15; 1 Peter 1:5.
** 1 John 1:7
*** Romans 8:1

by continually confessing our need for Jesus, and by making ourselves available to His Spirit to do as He pleases. How do we make ourselves available? We do this through the practice of spiritual disciplines.

Spiritual Habits

If you were raised in the church, you were likely taught that the way to be a good Christian—the way to follow Jesus—was to have a personal, daily quiet time.* Quiet time meant, well, quiet** for one, and also included Bible reading and prayer. You may have even been taught a certain time frame you should aim for—maybe thirty minutes or even an hour.

There were good intentions behind this messaging. Spiritual formation became a widely discussed and prioritized topic in the eighties. Churches were trying to make disciples, deepen people's knowledge of scripture, and nurture a personal relationship with Christ. Reading your Bible is vital to your spiritual health. Prayer is a crucial component of living a life of faith. Regularly engaging in those habits is essential to our spiritual well-being.

The problem with this well-intentioned messaging was that it turned spiritual disciplines into a checklist—something we did to feel Christian, or to set ourselves apart from those who weren't engaging in any spiritual disciplines, or even to judge our spiritual maturity. Then, as the '80s and '90s church kids grew up, it created a culture of guilty

---

* Every morning was godliest, but if you just couldn't set your alarm any earlier, then an evening quiet time would have to do. But the main message was: Get it done every day, and if not, feel guilty about it!

** I actually have a memory of trying to have my "quiet time" in a dry, empty bathtub. For some reason that felt like the quietest spot in my house, and I guess you get points for how quiet you can be?

millennial moms who can't figure out how on earth to have a daily
"quiet time" when they're unable to even shower or escape to the bathroom alone! (By the way, at what age do your children stop interrupting
your personal potty time? Asking for a friend . . .)

So, where does that leave us? If the spiritual disciplines you were
taught don't seem to fit your current life—or maybe you've never even
considered them—then what does it look like to grow spiritually in the
soil where God has planted you? Let's start by getting clear on what
spiritual habits are and what they aren't.

Spiritual Habits Are Not . . .

Spiritual habits are not a list of activities for us to check off so we can
pat ourselves on the back or tell ourselves we're being a good Christian.
They do not, I repeat, *do not* measure spiritual maturity. You can spend
an hour a day in the Bible, another hour on your knees in prayer, and
the entire day fasting, but you can still be angry, bitter, unkind, and
uncharitable. If you read the Bible for an hour but remember nothing,
apply nothing, and forget you even opened it until the next morning,
was it time with God or just time spent?

Spiritual habits are not, again, I repeat—this time in all caps—
ARE NOT a way to curry favor with God.

By the time I was sixteen years old, I had been a practicing Christian for twelve years. I was the senior pastor's firstborn child. By this
point, I was practically a teenage expert at being a Christian. I was sitting at the kitchen island, sharing with my mom some disheartening
mental and emotional issues I was wrestling with, when she stopped me.

"Hanna, do you know that there is nothing you can do that would
make God love you more?"

Silence.

"Do you know there is nothing you can do that would make God love you less?"

More silence.

Slowly, my brain began to take it in. WHAT?! I knew God loved me like He loved the whole world (hello, John 3:16), but somewhere deep down I believed the lie that if I did more for Him—if I read my Bible, if I prayed regularly, if I led worship and Bible studies, if I told my friends about Jesus, if I participated in the annual forty-eight-hour fast our youth group did—then He'd love me more. I also believed the flip side of that coin: If I didn't do all of those things, He'd love—or at least like—me less.

"Are you saying I could stop waking up early to read my Bible and God would still love me the same?"

"Yep." She smiled, eyebrows raised.

Challenge accepted, Mom.

For the first time in my entire life, I didn't read my Bible on a daily basis. In fact, I didn't pick it up at all for months.

Practicing spiritual habits will not make God love you more. He will not like you more. You will not curry favor or gain His approval more by doing them.

He loves you because He is Love. We might think He loves us because He created us in His image or because He has adopted us as His children, and while both of those things are true, He loves you because that is the essence of who He is. He doesn't love you because of who you are; He loves you because of who He is. In the same way, you have favor with God not because of anything you've done or could do, but because of what Jesus did on your behalf. Jesus essentially curried God's favor on our behalf. He did for us what we could never do for ourselves.

Spiritual Habits Are . . .

Dozens of books have been written on the practice of spiritual disciplines. Pick up three and you'll find eight different definitions.

"The Spiritual Disciplines are the *means* God uses to build in us an inner person that is characterized by peace and joy and freedom."

—RICHARD FOSTER[4]

"The Spiritual Disciplines are the *means* God uses for producing in us the needed transformation of heart and mind and soul."

—RICHARD FOSTER[5]

Spiritual Disciplines are "practices of heart, mind, and soul that place us before God."

—RICHARD FOSTER[6]

". . . they are opportunities for engaging with God."

—SHE READS TRUTH[7]

"They are exercises which equip us to live fully and freely in the present reality of God—and God works with us, giving us grace as we learn and grow."

—RENOVARÉ INSTITUTE[8]

They "are practices found in Scripture that promote spiritual growth."

—DONALD WHITNEY[9]

"Think of the Spiritual Disciplines as ways by which we can spiritually place ourselves in the path of God's grace and seek Him."

—DONALD WHITNEY[10]

Here's my definition: **Spiritual habits are intentional practices that help us know and love God, sustain fellowship with Him, and shape us to reflect His character.** The goal is not the habits themselves (and this is where we often get caught up); the goal is to be tethered to Jesus.

We practice spiritual habits as a way to put ourselves in a posture that allows Him to transform us. Spiritual habits help us live faithfully, no matter what our surrounding circumstances may be.

Too often, Christians believe that simply trying harder will make us more like Jesus, but that's not how transformation happens. John Ortberg said it's not by trying, but by training.[11] When we practice spiritual habits, we are training. When we read verses like Philippians 4:6 that say "don't be anxious" and think, *Okay! I just need to stop being anxious. I need to try harder to battle anxiety*—that is not the answer. Instead, regularly engaging in a variety of spiritual habits trains us and builds our spiritual muscles so that slowly but surely, anxiety no longer has a grip on us. We begin to experience peace and joy in place of worry or fear because we have been consistently spending time in the presence of Christ and have allowed His Spirit to transform us.

Spiritual Habits Help Us Know and Love God

When we open our Bibles and study God's Word, the point is not to simply learn more about the Bible. The point is to grow in our knowledge and understanding of God. Who is He? What does He love? What does He hate? What does He desire for His people? What is His plan?

We don't memorize scripture to keep track of how many verses we know. We memorize scripture so that the very Word of God is written deep down in our hearts. Spending time in prayer, solitude, practicing the Sabbath, pursuing community with other Christians—all of these spiritual disciplines help us know God more deeply and enjoy His presence more fully.

Since the beginning of time, God's invitation to man and woman has been to know Him, enjoy Him, serve Him, worship Him, and love Him. You're probably familiar with the New Testament story of the lawyer questioning Jesus on the greatest commandment:

> Jesus replied, "You must love the Lord your God with all your heart, all your soul, and all your mind." This is the first and greatest commandment (Matthew 22:37–38).

John recorded Jesus explaining that the way we show our love of Him is by obeying Him,* but our love of God is what propels us to obey. Jesus doesn't want obedience for the sake of obedience.** He wants our hearts; He wants our love.

It's no mistake that a frequently used analogy to describe our relationship with Christ is that of a bride and groom. God didn't accidentally create man and woman to love each other and commit to loving each other for life. God created marriage.*** The Triune God, who is Love, loves us and created us to love Him and one another. This is not rocket science, but somehow we miss this.

So, how do we begin to love someone on a human level? We spend time with them; we get to know them; we enjoy being around them. We

---

* See John 14:15, 21; John 15:10.
** See Hosea 6:6.
*** See Genesis 2:24–25.

begin sharing our whole selves with them. We trust them. We respect them. We grow in love and then commit to loving them through the ups and downs of life.

In a similar way, this is how we grow our love and affection for God. Through the practice of spiritual habits, we get to know Him, spend time with Him, enjoy His presence, learn to trust Him, revere Him, and ultimately love Him more deeply and wholeheartedly.

Spiritual Habits Help Us Sustain Fellowship with Him

Throughout scripture, God identifies Himself as our Father and us as His children. While this metaphor can be tricky for those who had abusive, neglectful, or absent earthly fathers, for anyone who becomes a parent, that illustration becomes technicolor, high-definition, and surround-sound. We viscerally understand what it means for a parent to love their child, to raise, train, and discipline them, and to be partly responsible for their maturation into adults.

However, there is a breakdown in this analogy. As a mom, my goal is to eventually launch full-fledged, independent adults. If I do my job correctly, my children should grow up in age and maturity, progressively becoming less and less dependent on me. They will no longer need me to help them get dressed, brush their teeth, feed them, or drive them places. They will advance in their decision-making abilities, emotional regulation, and wisdom, and be able to live, function, and ultimately thrive without me.

Some may say, "Oh, but you always need your mom." Well sure, in one sense, we all need our moms, but in reality, I will die someday, and more importantly, they *need* to be 100 percent capable of living a life apart from me in order to build their own lives, careers, and families.

But because we are children of God, God's goal is not to launch independent adults. His aim is not for us to be any less dependent on

Him than the first day we place our faith in Him. In fact, it's quite the opposite. His desire is to actually increase our dependency on Him. He doesn't want us to take one step throughout our day without Him. He doesn't want us making decisions without His guidance. While I need to raise adult children who are completely capable without me, God desires the exact opposite for His children.

The most mature child of God is not stronger, more independent, or more put together. The wise, aged, seasoned child of God knows they cannot move one muscle without depending on Christ.*

The consistent practice of spiritual habits keeps us in that place. It reminds us of our need for Him and keeps us in constant fellowship with Him.

After my several-month hiatus of "quitting" my morning Bible reading and prayer time, I found an old, unused Bible study, *Experiencing God* by Henry Blackaby, and threw it in the front seat of my 1991 Chevy Corsica. For about a year, I had been battling depression (not even knowing what depression was) while desperately trying to maintain an appearance of having it all together. I would drive to school, parallel park by 6:30 a.m.,** and sob in my car until it was time to fix my face and slip into my first class before the bell rang fifty minutes later. I was exhausted; I was miserable, and I just didn't know how to crawl out of it. But after I gave up my morning spiritual disciplines for the purpose of "pleasing God," I eventually began to wonder if there was something in those abandoned morning habits that could sustain or even heal me.

---

* It makes me think of the song lyrics "Lord, I need you, oh I need you. Every hour I need you." The mature Christ follower knows they need Jesus for every breath they take, every single moment of their day!

** Why so early, you might ask? Because the later you arrived, the farther you'd have to park from the school. Show up too late, and you'd be hoofing it from what felt like a different zip code. And listen—I was not about to power walk a mile to school when I was already trying to avoid gym class.

When I saw the title, *Experiencing God*, I thought: *That's exactly what I need. I need to experience God.*

Little by little, day by day, God met me in that maroon-upholstered Corsica with pink fuzzy dice hanging from the mirror. I still wept for hours each week. I still ached down to my bones, but I began to meet a God who offered comfort, peace, compassion, love, and strength. I started understanding habits like Bible reading, meditation, silence, solitude, and prayer as a way to get to know Him, connect with Him, be sustained by Him, and ultimately comprehend His love for me and love Him in return.

Spiritual Habits, Ultimately, Shape Us to Reflect Jesus

The Apostle Paul wrote to his protégé, Timothy: "train yourself for godliness" (1 Timothy 4:7, ESV). Spiritual habits are a way we submit ourselves to training that will result in being like Jesus.

But what does it mean to be godly or be like Jesus? Certainly, the goal isn't to become a first-century, Jewish thirty-year-old who travels around teaching the Torah in a mind-blowing way. Of course not.

God has created you uniquely—with your very own passions, proclivities, skills, and experiences. He has also placed you in your specific context—as macro as a woman in the twenty-first century in the Western world, down to the micro of your exact street address, the office building you sit in, the communities you're part of—including your kids' school or sports teams, your husband's job, or your own interests. That is the context God has purposely planted you in, and that's where He wants you to become like Him.

So, what does godliness look like? Our generation has a hard time with the words "holy" and "godly." They're Christian words that are overused and underexplained, and—let's be honest—they sound boring! But perhaps our best picture of godliness is in the person of Jesus Christ—and being like Jesus is far from uneventful! Just think about His life on earth! Being set apart (which is what "holy" means) as children of God who get to shine like stars in a crooked generation* sounds like a wild, adventure-filled life to me. Godliness and holiness just need a rebrand (a biblically rooted one) from the old, white-haired, stoic preacher we may picture.

Godliness looks like love and patience. It radiates kindness and humility but is not lacking in confidence. It's a gentle spirit, possessing great compassion. It's being quick to forgive and never holding grudges. It reflects abounding joy and peace that surpasses understanding. It chooses self-control and considers others' interests as more important than its own. Godliness speaks truth in love and cares deeply for the "least of these"—the mistreated, oppressed, and marginalized. It is marked by a non-anxious spirit. It walks in wisdom and discernment, smiles at the future, and sees people as God sees them.

When we practice spiritual habits with the right motives and goals, we are preparing ourselves like a sailboat. We hoist the sails, adjust their angles, and place our hands on the wheel to steer the rudder, all in an effort to align ourselves with our only power source—the wind. And as God's mighty Spirit fuels our meager efforts, we are able to move in the direction that He desires us to go.

Just as the sails and rudders are useless without the wind, spiritual habits themselves do not change us. They simply put us in a cooperating posture where transformation—by God's power—can occur.

The Work of the Holy Spirit

This brings us to Dallas Willard's second point of the golden triangle. Without the Spirit of God moving in and through us, spiritual habits are just Christian activities.

---

* See Philippians 2.

To pick back up in our Philippians 2 passage: "... for it is **God who works in you** to will and to act in order to fulfill his good purpose." His good purpose is for you to be like Jesus. In fact, earlier in chapter two, Paul says, "Have the same attitude as Jesus!" But don't miss the key ingredient: *It is God who works in you.* Not your willpower or self-discipline, not because you do all the right things in all the right ways. It is God working in you.

The Apostle Peter tells us that the practice of any spiritual gift (and I'd argue any spiritual practice) is to be done by the strength God supplies.*

Inner transformation is God's work, not ours, but we make ourselves available—we take on certain postures, we do certain things that allow Him access to our hearts, minds, and souls.

Forgive me if this isn't couth, but a proper analogy for this is the creation of life. If you've ever tried to get pregnant, or walked alongside a friend who has, it doesn't always just happen. You have to understand your cycle, know when you're ovulating, make sure you aren't using anything that could hinder those little swimmers getting to their goal. You must have sex at the very right time. I'm sure there are even more variables we could get into that we have control over, yet no matter how perfectly we work at making a baby, we don't actually have the power to create life. Only God is in the life-making business.

And only God is in the business of transforming lives.

Trials And Tribulations

The last point of Willard's triangle is "the faithful acceptance of everyday problems." The faithful what?! I'm sorry, Dr. Willard, I am not sure I like this idea very much.

---

* 1 Peter 4:11

For most of us, when life gets hard or when trouble comes our way, the first prayer that we utter to God is: "Fix it, Jesus!" Am I wrong? We pray and ask and beg that God would just change it, solve it, get us out of this mess. If you're like me, you also approach the Almighty God on His Throne with your best, most strategic ideas on how He could fix it. I've got plans for days, baby, that I have offered to God countless times, and frankly I'm still waiting for Him to use one of them!

Most of us move throughout life with the goal of being comfortable. We don't want trials. We don't want hardship. So, when those come our way, we send up our best prayers to convince God to remove us from the situation as quickly as possible. But God's goal for us is to grow, not be comfortable. While He is the Great Comforter, He is not interested in us being comfortable.

What do you know about grapes? One of my favorite passages of Jesus's teaching is found in John 15: "I am the vine; you are the branches. The one who remains in me—and I in him—bears much fruit, because apart from me you can accomplish nothing."*

Did you know that the grapevine, grape cluster, and vineyard are some of the most frequently used symbols in the Bible for God's chosen people—both Israel and the church—and His Kingdom? In fact, the people of Israel so closely identified with this symbol that at the entrance of the Holy Place in the Temple was a grapevine made of gold, with grape clusters the size of a man.[12] Wealthy families would even bring gold (shaped in the form of tendrils, grapes, and leaves) to be added to the vine.[13] This ornate design feature was a symbol of the nation of Israel, their connection to God, and His blessings of prosperity.

Grapes and vineyards were such a way of life for the cultures of the Ancient Near East and God's people for centuries (and they still are!)

---

* John 15:5, NET

that it just made good sense for the Spirit-inspired authors of the Bible and Jesus Himself to use them as a metaphor.

Why are we still talking about grapes, Hanna? Well, I'm so glad you asked.

When a veteran vinedresser goes to prepare a new plot of land for a vineyard, he digs up the soil and clears away some of the large stones, but he ensures there is a good distribution of pebbles, rock, flint, and gravel. It turns out that grapes need what you and I might determine to be horrible soil. In her book *Chasing Vines*, Beth Moore writes, "Rocks aren't simply obstacles the vinedresser has to contend with; they're something the grapes *require* in order to thrive."[14] If a grapevine is planted in rock-free soil and given all the sun and water she needs, she will inevitably grow larger and greener, but all she will produce are leaves. It is only when faced with a certain amount of hardship and struggle that the grapevine will actually produce grapes. Are you beginning to see why we're talking about grapes?

Jamie Goode, a wine columnist with a PhD in plant biology, explains, "Making the vines struggle generally results in better quality grapes. It's a bit like people. Place someone in a near-perfect environment, giving them every comfort and all that they could ever want to satisfy their physical needs, and it could have rather disastrous consequences for their personality and physique."[15]

Since God is the Creator of vines and grapes, and He even calls Himself the Vinedresser,* we can be certain that God has more expertise than any earthly wine guy. Which means He is definitely going to give us rocky soil conditions to help us produce fruit. So, back to Dallas Willard's golden triangle: A vital component of our spiritual maturity is our willingness to accept and endure the rocky soil that God gives us.

---

* John 15:1

This is why James and Peter say we can rejoice when we face trials,* and Paul says we can glory in our sufferings and even boast in our weaknesses.** The Great Vinedresser gives His beloved vines rocky soil so that we might become beautiful, fruit-bearing branches.

Looking back to Philippians 2 one more time, enduring trials *without grumbling or arguing* is how we *become blameless and pure* and *shine like stars in the sky.* It's through faithful endurance that we reflect God's glory.

Think about it. When you are all comfy-cozy and everything is going right in your world, do you feel like you need God? Do you draw close to Him? Do you depend on Him? Not usually or perhaps never. But when things get hard—when a family member hurts us, when the doctor delivers bad news, when we get laid off, when we feel crushed by the weight of the world—it is then that we reach out for God, and whether we like it or not, that's the soil He plants us in for our good and His glory.***

So, Who Shall We Become?

"Joy is the keynote of all the Disciplines," because "the purpose of the Disciplines is liberation from the stifling slavery [of] self-interest and fear."

—Richard Foster[16]

In *Chasing Vines*, Beth Moore paints a picture of the type of woman she wants to be in her last decade or two: "I want to age well and joyfully, keeping fiery faith and fiery love for Jesus, for the Scriptures, and for fellow human beings."[17]

---

* James 1:2–4, 1 Peter 1:6–7
** Romans 5:3–4, 2 Corinthians 12:9–10
*** Romans 8:28

She goes on to surmise that it is fullness of the Holy Spirit that allows those with decaying bodies to maintain a joyful heart. "It [the fullness of the Spirit and their attentiveness to His presence] also seems to leave a permanent mark. Their faces are lined with kindness, and their eyes sparkle and easily fill with tears upon the mention of the name of Jesus."[18]

When we practice spiritual habits a little at a time, day by day, year by year, the end result should be a ninety-year-old woman full of love, joy, and peace. She can be feisty and gentle, wise and hilarious, kind and candid. Our automatic nature is slowly transformed into someone who is quick to forgive, is slow to anger, has greater patience, isn't easily ruffled, finds peace amidst turmoil, and exudes joy in all circumstances. We will not become her by our efforts alone, but by the grace of God and the work of His Spirit continually transforming us little by little, day by day, year by year.

> God is doing the work . . . in our lives so that we might be brought into more intimacy with Him through the practice of the spiritual disciplines. And the joy of God, the presence of God, is the great reward in this process as we rely upon and depend upon His grace."
>
> —JUSTIN IRVING[19]

So, who do you want to be in the last decade of your life, and are you taking baby steps to become her?

One Last Thing

After we get into the science of habit formation in chapter two, the rest of this book will be about seven specific spiritual habits and how to begin practicing those habits in small, easy, but radically life-transforming ways. However, before we jump into the seven habits I've chosen, I want to take a moment to acknowledge that there are many lists of spiritual disciplines out there.

In *Celebration of Discipline*, Richard Foster discusses twelve disciplines divided into three categories. In his book *Spiritual Disciplines for the Christian Life*, Donald Whitney describes ten. Dallas Willard lists fifteen disciplines divided into two categories in *The Spirit of the Disciplines*. A She Reads Truth Bible study on spiritual disciplines lists twenty. John Mark Comer highlights nine. John Ortberg also writes about nine (but a different nine than Comer) in *The Life You've Always Wanted*. Yet, Adele Ahlberg Calhoun takes the cake with a whopping seventy-five disciplines in her *Spiritual Disciplines Handbook*.

The point here is that there isn't one agreed-upon or exhaustive list of spiritual disciplines. Some argue we should identify only activities we see in the Bible. Others say anything can be a spiritual discipline if it leads us toward wholeness in Christ. This argument leads some to include things like napping, walking, mentoring, truth-telling, and unplugging as spiritual disciplines.

I tend to lean toward the lists that are rooted in scripture, but I'm not about to get in a fight over it. That said, I chose a list of seven habits that have been the most helpful for me as a woman in her thirties and now forties who works multiple jobs while raising and homeschooling three kids, and (only by the grace of God) managing to keep her head on straight . . . most of the time. My hope is that these seven will also be just as fruitful for you.

In the remaining chapters, we'll look at:

Biblical Intake (including reading, studying, meditating, and memorizing)

Prayer

Solitude

Thanksgiving

Celebration

Friendship (traditionally called Community or Fellowship)

and Practicing the Presence of God

However, before we get into the basics of these seven disciplines, I want to help us reframe our perspective on spiritual disciplines to spiritual habits—no longer viewing them as lofty, time-consuming, backbreaking practices, but as small, continual habits that fit into our everyday lives, fueled by God's Spirit.

Chapter Review

- Spiritual habits are not activities for us to achieve, a way to measure spiritual maturity, or a way to curry favor with God.
- Spiritual habits are intentional practices that help us know and love God, sustain fellowship with Him, and shape us to reflect His character.

- Practicing spiritual habits puts us in a posture for God to transform us in godliness and holiness.
- Godliness and holiness simply mean becoming more like Jesus and shining like stars in a depraved generation. It's the farthest thing from boring.
- Dallas Willard taught the "golden triangle" of spiritual formation as: practicing the spiritual disciplines, the work of the Holy Spirit, and faithfully accepting and enduring trials and everyday problems.
- We will not passively become the person we want to be.

Your Homework*

- Go back to the several definitions of the spiritual disciplines on pages 18–19 and highlight the one that resonates most with you or put one into your own words.
- Picture yourself in your last decade of life. Who do you want to be? Write down a description of her. Leave nothing out.
- Take the Spiritual Health Check—a quick, no-judgment self-assessment of where you are right now. You can find this in Appendix A or download a PDF for free at hannaseymour.com/ESH. This is to help you identify where you want to begin creating new habits of spiritual disciplines to lead you down the path of the woman you want to become

---

* There is a free, printable workbook for you to use along with this book at hannaseymour .com/ESH.

CHAPTER TWO

So Long, "Go Big or Go Home"

"Do not despise these small beginnings, for the Lord rejoices to see the work begin, to see the plumb line in Zerubbabel's hand."

—The Prophet Zechariah[1]

I WAS THE SENIOR PASTOR'S DAUGHTER ATTENDING THE CHRISTIAN school affiliated with our church. I believed I was above the law and carried a sense of ownership over the campus that was probably not uncommon for a pastor's kid, but definitely not appropriate.

Every year in PE we had to run a timed mile and, though I played several sports, I was not a runner. Give me some sprints or a lap or two around the field, but please don't ask me to run for any length of time just for the sake of running. So, when it was my day to run the mile, I convinced two friends to join me by cutting corners just a bit. Instead of running around the school building multiple times, we'd cut into the building through a side door where no one would notice and slip out another exit, no one else the wiser. We weren't trying to make record-breaking time; we just didn't want to run that much. We did this for years. We "ran" a respectable eight-minute mile, and no one ever caught on.*

Fast forward to my mid-twenties, and something inside me—call it a quarter-life crisis, masochism, or just plain tomfoolery—decided I wanted to run a half-marathon. Up until this point, I had never run more than a mile** in my life, but I had the itch to accomplish something that was challenging. This, my friends, is the epitome of "go big or go home."

Since misery loves company, I convinced a friend to train with me. First, we began with a couch-to-5k plan, because as previously stated, I had never willingly run a day in my life unless it was toward a free Sonic corndog and tots, and then we faithfully followed Hal Higdon's half-marathon program for beginners. Hal told us what to do every single day for twelve weeks—and rain, snow, or shine, we obeyed. Some days were short runs, others long. Some days were strength training days, and there was one rest day a week. Not only did I successfully complete my training and run a half-marathon, I also continued running a variety of races over the next few years.

This is typically how we think of setting and achieving goals. We set our sights on a goal, and we train day by day, with effort, labor, and sweat, until we achieve that goal. And that's not wrong. When we want to accomplish something we've never done before, it requires a plan and faithful follow-through. It requires discipline. But if we don't lay a foundation of sustainable habits, we eventually fall off the wagon.

---

* On the off chance you're reading this—I'm so sorry, Mrs. Oster!

** I did eventually have to run a real, timed mile once I was in high school. We had an outdoor track that would have been fairly impossible to cut corners on, but by then I was also at a public school where my pastor's kid hubris and moxie were quickly humbled.

Three years after running my first half-marathon, I ran my last half-marathon. After several more years had passed, I had to attempt* a couch-to-5k program again because I was so out of running shape. I was no longer a runner, but every so often, I'd still catch myself saying I wanted to run one more half-marathon before I hit forty. Yet I never did. My fortieth birthday came and went, and I still have absolutely no desire to ever run a half-marathon again.

So what happened? I went from a cheating mile runner to a highly motivated and disciplined half-marathon runner to a zero-interest, won't-do-it-unless-someone-is-chasing-me-with-a-knife kind of runner.**

There are multiple issues with the "go big or go home" mentality, and we see them all at play in my rendezvous with running. First, while my audacious goal worked for a while (a few years!), my motivation to continue running eventually dwindled. When there wasn't a race to train for, I lost focus and drive. Second, being a runner—especially a long-distance one (if you call 13.1 miles long-distance, which I do, thank you very much)—wasn't really a sustainable lifestyle for me. It required too much of a time commitment in my daily routine. Third, while I sometimes enjoyed it, there were many times I didn't. I just never fell in love with running, and when you don't love doing something it gets harder and harder to stay motivated to keep at it. Fourth, and most importantly, my relationship with running was about setting and achieving goals—like completing certain races and hitting specific target times. It was an outcome-based result.

In his book *Atomic Habits*, James Clear argues that goal-setting is getting us nowhere, and instead of focusing on outcome-based results (running marathons, losing weight, reading a certain number of books

---

* I say *attempt* because I don't believe I successfully completed it.
** Not even for the Sonic corndog and tots anymore, because let's be honest: That post-forty metabolism doesn't play fair.

each year), we need to look at our daily habits and consider how those are naturally leading to our outcomes.[2]

You've likely heard the Annie Dillard quote "How we spend our days is, of course, how we spend our lives. What we do with this hour, and that one, is what we are doing."[3] This is the same idea James Clear gets across: The small habits we do over and over don't just create the outcomes of our lives; they actually create who we are. Our habits form our identity.

Instead of creating outward behavior-based or outcome-based goals, we need to create identity-based ones. "The goal is not to read a book, the goal is to become a reader. The goal is not to run a marathon, the goal is to become a runner. The goal is not to learn an instrument, the goal is to become a musician."[4]

The ultimate problem with my running goal was that the goal was never to become a runner. It was never about forming an identity. It was only about achieving external behavior.

The same is true when practicing spiritual habits. You may have attempted to accomplish certain goals in the past—read the Bible in a year, use a daily prayer journal, memorize a certain number of verses, write five things you're grateful for before bed, pray with your spouse every night, fast for a period of time—but did you become a Bible reader? Did you become a person who loves God and His Word? Did you grow into a woman who stays connected to God through prayer? Did God shape you into a person who looks more like Jesus and less like the world? Did your love for God and others increase?

While spiritual habits are things we do, they cannot simply be that. If they are—and many of us have experienced this—we eventually stop doing them. We lose energy and motivation. What we were doing wasn't sustainable for the long haul.

I f I know how you spend your time then I know what might become of you."

—JOHANN WOLFGANG VON GOETHE

From Achievement to Identity

What if we stopped worrying about these massive outcome-based goals surrounding spiritual habits and instead started with the question: Who do I want to become, and what small spiritual habits can I start to help me get there?

When we approach spiritual habits from an outcome-based, goal-oriented posture, not only are we setting ourselves up for failure, but we can end up looking a lot like the Pharisees of Jesus's day. And what did He call them? White-washed tombs. They may have looked holy on the outside, but just beneath the surface they were rotting, filled with death, decay, and a terrible stench.

Jesus doesn't want our obedience for the sake of obedience. He doesn't want us to simply do the right things because we are disciplined enough to do them. He wants our hearts. He wants us to walk with Him, day in and day out. He wants us to depend on Him.

And this, I believe, is the crux of redefining spiritual disciplines as habits.

We can't approach spiritual disciplines as something we achieve by our own determination, motivation, commitment, willpower, or the sweat of our brow. Instead, we are invited to live a life of faith in which we are continually reminded of God's love and presence throughout our ordinary days. We can practice small habits that reconnect us to Him over and over so that we can be sustained by His Spirit to accomplish His will.

We also can't practice spiritual habits with the goal being accomplishment. We shouldn't read our Bible, pray, worship, volunteer, or engage in any other practice to check a box. The reason to read the Bible is to know God better. The goal of prayer is to spend time in His presence, to align our hearts with His, and to listen and wait for God's Spirit to lead us. We practice spiritual habits so that they shape our identity.

Romans 12:2 says, "And do not be conformed to this world, but be transformed by the renewing of your mind, so that you may prove what the will of God is, that which is good and acceptable and perfect" (NASB). We are transformed moment by moment, day by day, into who God created us to be when we practice spiritual habits.

James Clear writes, "A habit is a routine or behavior that is performed regularly—and, in many cases, automatically."[5] While calling a behavior "automatic" might make it seem unintentional or thoughtless—and therefore not very spiritual—don't you want your spiritual habits to be automatic? When I fold laundry, I want to automatically begin praying for the owner and wearer of said laundry. As I close my laptop at the end of the workday, I want to automatically start reflecting and thanking God for a few ways I saw Him at work that day. When I wash dishes and move my hands over dirty pots and pans, I want to naturally begin practicing the presence of God. When I turn on the coffee machine, I want my automatic response to be looking over at my open Bible and reading or meditating on a few verses. When I get hit in the gut with fear or anxiety, I want to immediately turn to the Father and ask Him for help and guidance. I want my spiritual habits to be like breathing. Don't you? It's so automatic, we don't even think about it unless we've stopped! Just like breathing, spiritual habits should be the sustaining force to our very livelihood.

One of the most encouraging insights from the science of habit formation is that the reason we fail to accomplish our goals actually has nothing to do with our inability to be disciplined or have enough willpower. We fail because we have been incorrectly taught how to create habits in the first place. We've been given the wrong set of tools and instructions, but then we blame ourselves for not being able to put the Ikea desk together. So, if you've tried to read your Bible every day, or pray for a set time each morning, or practice the Sabbath, and you eventually failed to maintain those rhythms, the science of habit formation says, "It's not your fault!" Let's take a look at what the science of habit formation says about creating habits that stick.

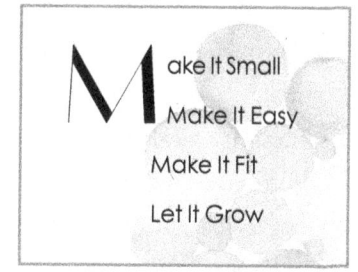

ake It Small
Make It Easy
Make It Fit
Let It Grow

There are four main steps to how we are going to create sustainable, lifelong habits of spiritual disciplines. The first is to make it small.

Make It Small

Dr. BJ Fogg, a Stanford professor and behavioral scientist, says the way to begin a new habit is to create one that you can accomplish in less than thirty seconds. James Clear says you need to be able to accomplish your new habit in two minutes or less. Regardless, you take the larger behavior or identity you want, and you scale it down to the easiest, quickest win. Fogg calls these Tiny Habits. Clear calls them Atomic Habits. As previously mentioned, I'm calling them Seed Habits.

In his book *Tiny Habits*, Dr. Fogg gives the example of how he has always wanted to be a person who regularly flosses his teeth. Every six months, after his routine cleaning, he'd be determined to start flossing every night. His motivation would be high for the first few nights, but then he'd lose steam. Flossing is boring and annoying anyway.*

One day, Fogg realized he needed to create a Tiny Habit for flossing. Instead of aiming to floss all of his teeth every night (for he had consistently proven to himself this wasn't a habit he could maintain), he decided his Tiny Habit was to simply floss one tooth each night. For many nights, that was all he did—one tooth. You may be thinking, *What on earth was that accomplishing?!* But in fact, it was accomplishing something vital: He was mastering the habit of showing up. Eventually, he started flossing more teeth, and pretty soon he was consistently flossing his entire set of pearly whites—not just at night but in the morning too!**

Yet even now, occasionally Dr. Fogg just doesn't feel like flossing, so he only flosses one tooth. He doesn't feel bad for only flossing one tooth, because he's still practiced his habit, and flossing just one tooth is enough to keep the habit alive.

That is what we're going for here: keeping habits alive, sustainable, and continual—day after day.

Now, you may be thinking: *That's a cute (and also weird) story, but that just doesn't seem applicable to most life habits. If I want to become a person who is physically fit, I need to be working out regularly. So how on earth could thirty seconds or even two minutes of working out (can we even call that working out?!) benefit me or get me to that goal?*

---

* Apologies to my dentist friends and family.
** I actually love flossing my teeth at night, but you lost me at twice a day!

I was about a year postpartum after my third child and was desperate to get back into a regular rhythm of working out and taking care of my body. I had recently begun a seminary program in which I had to identify personal goals as part of a self-leadership class. I was embarrassingly aware of how poorly I had been taking care of my physical health, but I couldn't imagine a world where I would be able to begin regularly exercising. I already woke up before the sun, my entire day was full, and then once the kids were in bed, I was back in my office studying for class.

I signed up for a six-week session where a fitness and nutrition coach beat me into shape, and while I hung in there fairly well, it felt excruciatingly hard (which meant I didn't enjoy it), and it was in no way sustainable. Instead of feeling inspired and motivated to continue prioritizing my physical health (as the program had promised), I finished the six weeks feeling completely defeated and resigned to the idea that I just wouldn't work out regularly until after finishing my seminary degree.

Then, I heard a podcast with three fitness trainers discussing the habit of simply showing up. They talked about starting small with a workout plan, and how even if you didn't feel like working out, you could just step into the gym for a minute. Tell yourself you only have to do one exercise, and then if you want to go home after that, you're free to go. I thought, *I can do that. I can carve out a few minutes after I finish studying each morning, walk into our home gym, and do one set of squats or lunges. That seems doable.*

I realized that even working out a few minutes a day for five or six days a week added up to a lot more than zero. It was a baby step, but I was cultivating the habit of showing up.

Those same trainers have a workout plan that only takes fifteen minutes a day. After doing a few minutes of squats, lunges, crunches, or pull-ups daily for a few weeks, I thought, *A fifteen-minute daily workout plan? I can probably do that.* And if I felt tired or unmotivated, I knew I had permission to just do one exercise because they said so!

After twelve weeks of consistently working out for fifteen minutes or less, I wanted more. Slowly but surely, the habit of showing up grew into something more, something I looked forward to. I learned how to carve out more time in my mornings because I wanted to. It didn't feel like a drudgery. It didn't feel hard. But I only got there by starting small, making it easy, making it fit, and slowly letting it grow.

> The point is not to do one thing. The point is to master the habit of showing up."
>
> —JAMES CLEAR[6]

Are you going to open your Bible and read for thirty minutes every day for the rest of your life? Maybe, but probably not if that seems like a giant leap for you in your current season. But what if your initial "make it small" Seed Habit was to read one verse a day? Could you do that consistently? I bet you could. Then, what if that habit slowly, over time, grew to thirty minutes a day? Just like with my workout routine, you'll find yourself faithfully reading your Bible for more time than you thought you could because you started small and grew to love it. But on the mornings when you wake up late or get thrown off your normal rhythm, you'll just read one verse. And that's perfectly fine, because one verse is all it takes to keep your daily habit of Bible intake alive.

By the power of Christ's Spirit, we know that even one sentence of

God's Word is enough to do something in our hearts, minds, and lives. Scripture says His Word never returns void. It doesn't say it has to be read for at least thirty minutes. It simply never—even only one tiny verse—returns void!*

I'm not telling you to hack the spiritual life here or create one hundred tiny spiritual habits in your day so you can check a box or feel religious. I want to show you how planting tiny seeds and scattering them throughout your day will take root, sprout, and blossom—some into explosive wildflowers and others into tall and sturdy oak trees. These Seed Habits will grow into a garden of spiritual maturity that will result in a deeper fellowship with God, an overwhelming love of Jesus, and an irresistible joy, peace, contentment, and faith that others will notice.

Starting small is the antithesis of the "go big or go home" mentality. The problem with that mentality, as you likely know, is that a lot of times, we just end up going home. We want to work out more, eat healthier, lose weight, drink more water, sleep better, save money, pay off our debt, start our own business, write a book, start a podcast, grow a home garden, learn a new skill or hobby, pray more frequently, grow in our spiritual maturity, and more. But when we create big goals, with that "go big or go home" mentality, the first time we fail we throw in the towel. If we don't see our desired progress, we lose steam. To paraphrase James Clear: We've fallen for the lie that massive success requires massive action.

Not too long ago, a friend of mine confessed her desire to read three chapters of the Bible a day, but many days she doesn't read at all because she only has a few spare scattered minutes, and even one chapter feels out of reach. "What's wrong with just reading for a minute or

---

* See Isaiah 55:11.

two throughout your day?" I asked. This is exactly the "go big or go home" mentality rearing its ugly head. In her mind, if she can't read at least one chapter, she might as well not even try. But what is better? A few minutes of Bible intake throughout your day, or none at all? We know the right answer, yet how many times have we all felt that way?

Clear writes, "The difference a tiny improvement can make over time is astounding. Here's how the math works out: if you can get one percent better each day for one year, you'll end up thirty-seven times better by the time you're done."[7] In his book, Clear explains how an airplane from Los Angeles to New York City can be taken off route and will land in Washington, DC, if the pilot adjusts the heading only by 3.5 degrees. What seems like the most insignificant change will result in a destination difference of 225 miles over a several-hour flight. How often in life are we making the tiniest change that over the years accumulates into a very different final destination than we hoped for?

Tiny Changes in Our Daily Routines Gain Momentum

Have you ever heard about the snowball effect? The snowball effect is a psychological concept that explains how small actions at the beginning can cause bigger and bigger actions, ultimately resulting in a huge change. Visualize a tiny snowball beginning at the top of a mountain and rolling down, gradually accumulating. It eventually becomes a massive avalanche. I learned this idea from the Ramsey Solutions team, who use it to help people get out of debt. When facing multiple debts (student loans, car loans, credit cards, you name it), you might think the best way to tackle debt is to go from your largest debt to your smallest debt. Go big or go home, am I right?! While that may save you interest money in the long run, the Ramsey folks preach that the snowball effect is the way to go because you get easy wins up front, which then create more and more incentive and momentum for you to crush your largest debts.*

Make It Easy

So first, we start small. Next, we make it easy.

Whatever small habit you want to cultivate, you need to make it as easy as possible for yourself to accomplish. There's a lot of psychology behind why those two elements are important, but it can be boiled down to this: We need a really easy win, and we need the path of least resistance. When we succeed, when we do the thing we set out to do (even if it's only flossing one tooth or doing five squats), our brain releases dopamine. When the reward center of our brain is triggered, it makes us feel good about ourselves, which leads us to repeat the habit again. Taking the habit you want to cultivate and distilling it into a small and easy action allows you to be successful immediately and grow from there. We'll get into the nitty-gritty of what this looks like for spiritual disciplines in the chapters to come, but to give you a more generic idea:

If you want to get in shape—instead of joining a gym or vowing to work out six days a week—you decide to do three push-ups every time you flush the toilet. If you want to drink more water—instead of buying a gallon water jug and solemnly swearing to drink it all in a day—you begin by taking one sip of water every morning when you first walk into the kitchen. If you want to read more books—instead of setting a goal to read twenty-four books that year—you commit to opening a book before you go to bed every night.

---

* Dave says, "It's a mental problem at this point, not a math problem." Quick wins and seeing progress are way more motivational than slowly chipping away at your largest debt.

I have yet to meet a Christian who doesn't want to read their Bible more. Every person who genuinely wants to live a life of faith and follow Christ wants to read their Bible more. Plenty of well-meaning friends have said, "Eureka! I know how I'm going to create a lifelong habit of reading the Bible! I shall read the Bible in a year!" (Okay, none of my friends talk like that, but honestly life would be more interesting if they did.) While I'm sure you know someone who completed that "go big or go home" goal on the first try, most of us don't make it past Leviticus. BECAUSE IT'S HARD (and also, *Leviticus, am I right?!*). It's challenging to slog through the Old Testament for twenty minutes a day when we've never practiced simply opening our Bibles every day. (And I do literally mean just opening them.)

You can make this habit way smaller by deciding you're going to read one verse or for one minute. Something simple. You make it easy by leaving an open Bible in the location where you plan to do this small, easy Bible reading. Maybe you have a reading plan printed out or something to remind you exactly what you're going to read each day. Because nothing is worse than saying, "I'm going to read my Bible every day!" but then not having a place or plan to do it. You've got to find your Bible. Then you have to decide what to read. Do you just open it up and play Bible roulette and hope you land on an inspiring verse like: "Be still and know that I am God" (Psalm 46:10, NIV) and not "'Very well,' he said, 'I will let you bake your bread over cow dung instead of human excrement'" (Ezekiel 4:15, NIV)? No, you make this easy by predetermining the plan and leaving a Bible out on the table, open to the page you'll read from.

To give a nonspiritual example, every morning I "tumble out of bed and stumble to the kitchen, pour myself a cup of ambition, and yawn and stretch and try to come to life."[8] We have a frugally bougie, super-automatic espresso machine, but there are many mornings when I go to press the "on" button and the error light shines—not enough water, not enough beans, the grounds container needs to be emptied—and my soul cries because I need that coffee, and I need it now.

One day it dawned on me—*How can I make this easier?* So, I created a new habit. Right before I head to bed, I check the machine. I make sure it has plenty of water and beans, and I check the drip tray and grounds container in case they need to be emptied. Now, when I wake up in the morning, my coffee ritual is as easy as pie. If this small habit of preparation can help me get that sip of nectar to my mouth more easily each morning, surely there are ways we can smooth the path for the much more important nourishment of our souls.

Make It Fit

We've made our desired lifelong habit small. We've made it easy. Now, perhaps the most crucial element—we need to make it fit.

This means I won't tell you to set your alarm earlier so you have time to read your Bible or pray. I won't push you to squeeze gratitude or solitude into an already-packed schedule. I won't ask you to sacrifice anything or carve out extra time you don't have. *Making it fit* means thinking through your most ordinary day and identifying the hundreds of habits you already perform consistently—most without ever thinking about them. Then, following a framework developed by BJ Fogg,[9] you create a formula that goes like this:

After I (insert habit you already do), I will (insert new Seed Habit).

Making a new habit stick requires us to consider our existing habits and identify the best prompt to trigger the new Seed Habit. At the end of this chapter, your homework will be to write down every habit you already do daily (or often several times a day). Here are a few to get you started.

Every Day, I . . .

—Turn off my alarm clock

—Put my slippers on

—Use the restroom (so many times!)

—Walk into the kitchen

—Make coffee

—Walk into my office

—Turn on the lamp

—Sit in my chair

—Walk out of my office

—Brush my teeth

—Make my bed

—Put on workout clothes

—Grab my phone off the charger

—Walk into the garage/gym

—Walk back into the house

—Empty the dishwasher

These are obviously not step-by-step details of my morning routine. I could get even nittier and grittier if I wanted to. I do all of the above in the first two hours of my day, so just think about how long this list could be if we detailed every hour of our normal day.

Using our formula above, here is a Seed Habit I've been working on:

After I put my slippers on, I will say a quick prayer of gratitude and submission.

I am not naturally wired to be a morning person. I would sleep in every day until 9:00 a.m. if I could, and I still would prefer not to speak to anyone for the first hour I'm awake. But as a mom and a woman who wants to live well, I have to wake up early. So, years ago, I decided to start saying, "I'm becoming a morning person." Little did I know the science of habit formation says this is exactly how to approach my desired identity-based outcome. I want to be a morning person, so I have dozens of tiny habits I do every day that feed into that identity, and slowly but surely, year after year, I am becoming more and more of a morning person. I don't know if I'll ever wake up with a giant smile on my face and leap out of bed like a kid on Christmas morning, but after years of small habits in place, I can truthfully say I have fallen in love with the early morning hours. In fact, I now prefer early morning to late evening. *I am a morning person!* (She says hesitantly, but confidently.)

So, my "Slippers Prayer" feeds into my identity-based outcome of being a morning person, and it also feeds into my long-term desire to be a woman whose first thought in the morning is the Lord and whose first action is connecting with Him.

The prayer is simply: "Good morning, Lord. Thank you for a new day. It's Your day; help me to live for You. It's going to be a great day!" And then my brain tells my face to smile, but my success rate on that is marginally lower than saying the prayer itself. But, hey—I'm a work in progress! I just want to be an eighty-year-old who immediately thinks of Jesus when she opens her eyes every morning and then SMILES. That's my long-term, identity-based goal! With God's help, I'm confident I'll get there.

That habit is small; it's easy, and I've made it fit by using my slippers as the cue.

Make It Stickier Faster: The 7x Method

I was worried this was a habit I wouldn't be able to make stick. My brain is so dead tired in the morning that I thought, *There is no earthly way I'm going to remember to do this.* Here's a silly but research-backed hack to make your new habit stick faster: the 7x Method. The night before I started my new morning prayer habit, I set out my slippers, sat on my bed, and then immediately got back up, put on my slippers, and said, "Now I'm going to say my prayer." (In hindsight, I should have said my new prayer—that would have made this habit even stickier.) Then I repeated the whole routine, seven times in a row.

I was totally anticipating my husband catching me in the act and curiously staring at me while I completed the practice ritual, but mercifully, I was saved from that minor embarrassment.

Research shows that if we do these crash-course habit practice sessions seven to ten times, we significantly increase our chances of remembering the new habit and making it stick.[10] I chose seven because it already felt like a lot of times, and seven is God's holy number. So if it's good enough for Him, it's good enough for me.*

When I was working with the survey results that I mentioned earlier in the book, I saw the desire women had to prioritize their spiritual health, but they struggled with finding the time, effort, or resources to do so. Part of my class project was to highlight a need revealed by the survey and create a Biblical response. I knew whatever I chose to create had to be super small and easy for these women to use. So, I created an email newsletter called *The Weekly One*. It's one verse, one quote, and one question written to encourage readers in their walk with Jesus. I keep it short enough that you can read it while waiting for your cup of coffee to brew. So, if I wanted to pretend that was your habit, your formula would be:

After I **press "brew" on the coffee machine**, I will **open *The Weekly One* and read it**.

It's small, easy, and it fits.

As you may have noticed, I've used the word *formula* a few times to describe the way you are going to plan for our new Seed Habit. I like this term because we need to think of our habits as formulas that we experiment with. They take repetition, practice, observations, and tweaks until we get them honed in to produce the outcome we want each time.

So, if you create your first formula and begin trying it out (maybe

---

* I hope you know me well enough by now to recognize that I'm lovingly joking and not being disrespectfully irreverent.

you even did a "make it stickier faster" 7x practice session), but it's just not working—remember that this is an ongoing process. It's an evolving formula until it sticks. You may need to go back, rethink your formula, and make some tweaks. Perhaps your prompt isn't right. Maybe it's the wrong moment in the day. Maybe your prompt isn't clear enough or you need to break down your prompt even more. Perhaps the prompt isn't the problem at all, but your habit is not small or easy enough.

When my kids started school this year, I wanted to create a habit of praying over them before they headed out the door. I envisioned we'd circle up in the kitchen and stack hands in the middle like a sports team. I'd pray over them and then release them into the wild. *TEAM SEYMOUR!*

I was able to pull this off once, maybe twice, but I realized our mornings were just a little too chaotic. We were never all in the kitchen—much less the same vicinity—when it was time for my husband to take our two sons to their homeschool tutorial. He was flying out of our bedroom, the boys were upstairs, downstairs, or outside. Their sister could be anywhere, and I was usually in the garage working out.

As I was researching for this book, it dawned on me: *You wanted to create a habit of praying over your kids before they left for school, but it's not working at all because you haven't found the right fit or prompt in your morning routine.* So I tweaked it. You know what always happens before my husband takes our boys to school? They find me to give me a hug. Every time. You know what my new prompt is? When they are hugging me, I pray over them. Sometimes out loud, sometimes silently. Sometimes it's a one-second prayer, "Lord, be with them!" and sometimes it's a little longer with some specificity for their day. But by tweaking the prompt, I made that floundering habit stick really quickly. Then, when I take my daughter to her mother's-day-out program, I pray for her out loud as I hold her hand and we walk from the car to her classroom. It's become such a habit that if I hesitate, she reminds me. "Mom, aren't you going to pray for me?"*

My beautiful, clear-eyes-full-hearts-can't-lose vision of a family huddle and corporate blessing didn't pan out for this particular season of life, but I always have that quick moment of prayer for my kids each morning, and that's what I'm after! I care that it happens more than how it looks. It matters to me that I get the moment to invite God into our day and remind myself that God is looking after my children better than I ever could, and my kids know that their mom covers them in prayer every time they go out into the world.

A final note about prompts before we move on. When you think about the Seed Habit you're wanting to commit to your regular routine, make sure you are matching your desired frequency of the habit to the frequency of the prompt. For instance, if you only want to do something once or twice a day, you might match it with brushing your teeth or doing the dishes. If you want to do something several times a day, you might match it with using the restroom, filling up your water bottle, washing your hands, or waiting at a red light.

Celebrating and Dopamine

Before we land the plane on creating Seed Habits and how to let them grow, I want to acknowledge there's another piece to the science of habit formation that feels a bit awkward when we apply it to the practice of spiritual habits. The science of habit formation says that when we are working on a new habit, we will have more success if we find a way to release dopamine in our brains.

Conversations about dopamine have dominated airwaves and algorithms in recent years, so you're probably already familiar with the

---

* It's amazing what a three-year-old can remember when she wants to.

gist of it. In brief, dopamine is a neurotransmitter that impacts a lot of things, but primarily it gives you feelings of pleasure, satisfaction, and motivation. So, when we are practicing our new Seed Habits, if we can trick our body into releasing dopamine in the reward center of our brain, we will be motivated to do that habit again. BJ Fogg has defined this step in his habit formation method as Celebration. He counsels his clients to take a quick moment to celebrate themselves after they accomplish their Tiny Habit. So, when Dr. Fogg flossed one tooth, he'd look into the mirror, smile, make his hand into a V shape, and say, "Victory!" He celebrated himself for doing his Tiny Habit, which released dopamine, and essentially hacked his brain into being more motivated to do that Tiny Habit the next day. Once a habit has become sticky, the need to celebrate drops off, but research shows if you celebrate in the early stages, it vastly accelerates and improves your chances of success.

However, if I told you to give yourself a high-five or do a mini-celebration dance after you completed your Seed Habit of reading one Bible verse in the morning—that feels a little weird, right? It feels wrong to celebrate ourselves after practicing a spiritual discipline. *Good job, Hanna! Way to go reading a verse of God's revealed Word to us. Wahoo!*

Still, I think we can reframe this biblically and find that it can fit with our new spiritual habits. At the end of Paul's letter to the church in Philippi, he says, "Rejoice in the Lord always; again I will say, rejoice" (Philippians 4:4). In the just 104 verses that comprise his letter, Paul uses the Greek word for joy or rejoice fourteen times. The words *joy*, *rejoice*, or *joyful* are translated 430 times in the English Standard Version of the Bible. That's a lot of rejoicing.

The difference between a worldly celebration and a biblical one centers around the who and what. We'll dig into this much more in chapter six, but we are commanded to celebrate what God has done. When we decide we want to increase our habits and practices of the spiritual disciplines, how could that not please God? When we show up for a new spiritual habit—even a Seed Habit of reading one Bible verse each morning—I believe God is pleased, and we can celebrate that. Instead of saying, *Wahoo! I did it!* we can say, *Wahoo! Thank you, Lord! Your Spirit reminded me to do that, and your Word never returns void! YAY!* You can cut out the *wahoo* and *yay* if that feels disingenuous to you, but I think we can smile and say, "*Thanks, Lord*" and feel glad—even proud—of what we just did.

I recall a time when my dad was congratulating me on a job well done. I responded, "Oh, well . . . um . . . thank you? But I mean, God really did it!" My dad put his hand on my shoulder, looked me in the eyes, and said, "Yes, of course, but God uses people too." We can give God all the credit for every momentous success and accomplishment in our lives—and we should! But we also shouldn't minimize the fact that God uses people, and in order to be an effective vessel, you have to be obedient to Him and willing to work! So whether you write a book (*To God be the glory!*) or run a marathon (*I can do all things through Christ who strengthens me!*) or you choose to read the Bible while your coffee brews instead of scrolling on your phone (*Thanks for reminding me, God!*) or you practice a moment of solitude at the end of your workday (*Thanks for giving me that time, Lord!*)—you still had to make a choice. You still had to take action, and you still had to respond in obedience to Him. We can celebrate what God has done in and through us and also be encouraged about the part we played.

Let It Grow

Phew! Are you still with me? We're almost done with our crash course in creating sustainable habits that will lead us on our path of lifelong growth. Our final step to creating sticky habits is to simply let it grow. If you start with a Seed Habit of reading one verse or one minute of scripture every morning, that is incredible! You will have read 365 verses or 365 minutes of scripture in a year that you would not have read otherwise. That is something to celebrate! If a plane can be diverted 225 miles with a 3.5-degree change, what can 365 minutes of God's Word do in our lives? It gives me goosebumps! His Word and Spirit are so much more powerful than a Boeing 747 turbofan engine! (They actually have four!) At the same time, while one minute a day is great, we still want to grow that Seed Habit, right?

Sometimes growth looks like the time or amount increased. So, you bump your Bible reading time from one minute to five, or five to ten. Other times it means we add a similar habit at another point in our day. You find another moment you can read a little more scripture—maybe it's when you sit down to eat lunch or dinner, or right before bed. Sometimes it means we add a new but different Seed Habit on top of the last one. For this example, maybe you read for one minute and then pray for one minute or work on Bible memorization or meditation for one minute.

If this step feels a little loosey-goosey to you, you're not wrong. Letting it grow takes us back to the science-experiment nature of creating habits. We find what works; we take hold of the areas we want to keep growing or start pursuing a few new areas. The science of habit formation tells us that a natural process of growth will occur. We don't have to buckle down and find more willpower or motivation to grow these things. Good, sticky habits that lead us down the path we want to be on beget more good, sticky habits that further propel us down the road of growth. And that's just what the science says! We also have the promises of God, which assure us that when we obey Him, walk in His ways, and seek His face, He ignites our passion and deepens our faith.* The beautiful thing about creating spiritual habits is that we have the Spirit of God working on our behalf to grow our desire of connection with Him, to grow our appetite for practicing spiritual habits, and to increase our awareness of His presence and work in our lives.

Chapter Review

- We can stop setting "go big or go home" goals for spiritual growth.
- We can start by identifying who we want to become, and then create Seed Habits that will help us grow into the person we want to be.
- The four steps to a sustainable habit are:

  - Make it small
  - Make it easy
  - Make it fit
  - Let it grow

- When beginning a new habit, a moment of celebration is appropriate and helpful in making our habits stick.
- Our Seed Habits are like science experiments: They take repetition, observations, and tweaks to get them to consistently produce our desired outcome.
- The formula** for a Seed Habit is: After I _____, I will _____.

---

* See John 14:23, Deuteronomy 5:33, Proverbs 16:20, Psalm 37:18, and I could go on.
** Again, created by BJ Fogg.

Your Homework

- Set a timer for two minutes and freewrite everything that comes to mind when answering the prompt: *Who do I want to become?* You may find it easier to imagine yourself ten, twenty, or thirty years from now and then answer that question.
- Spend five minutes and write down every daily habit you already do. You'll come back to this list in future chapters once you're ready to create some Seed Habits.
- BONUS POINTS (for my overachievers): Teach one person the four steps to creating a sticky habit and anything else you want to remember from the chapter. (Hint: Use the chapter review to help you!)

One Final Note

Now that you've wrapped your arms around the big ideas of spiritual habits and how to make them small and easy, fit them into your day, and let them grow, this is the point where you are free to jump to a specific chapter should you feel compelled. I wrote this book for the busy woman, so l can't blame you if you don't have the time or energy to read it from cover to cover. If that's you, feel free to jump to the chapter you are most drawn to. If you want to start creating one to three Seed Habits within the discipline of solitude because you need it in the worst way—be my guest and flip to chapter six. This book will always be here for you to come back to when you're ready to start experiencing God through a different spiritual habit.

CHAPTER THREE

Devour the Bible

"Let us treat scripture like scripture—like God speaking to us."
—Augustine of Hippo (354–430)[1]

While helping Billy Graham write his memoir, Jerry Jenkins asked Graham about his habit of reading the Bible.

> "Say you miss a day or two," Jenkins said. "How do you get back to your routine?"
> "Miss a day or two? I don't think I've ever done that."
> "You never miss?"
> "I told you. This is my spiritual food. I would no more miss this than a regular meal."[2]

Growing up, I remember many times when my mom would suddenly realize that she forgot to eat lunch. I absolutely cannot relate. Yes, I have had days so busy I never stop to feed myself, but I have never *forgotten* (in fact, I am acutely aware), and by late afternoon my body is screaming at me to remedy the situation.

Several times throughout scripture, we see the metaphor of eating God's Word:

> When I discovered your words, I devoured them (Jeremiah 15:16).

> Son of man, eat what I am giving you—eat this scroll! Then go and give its message to the people of Israel (Ezekiel 3:1).

> How sweet your words taste to me; they are sweeter than honey (Psalm 119:103).

> I had to feed you with milk, not with solid food, because you weren't ready for anything stronger (1 Corinthians 3:2).

> Like newborn babies, you must crave pure spiritual milk so that you will grow into a full experience of salvation (1 Peter 2:2).

> Taste and see that the Lord is good (Psalm 34:8).

Most famously, Jesus said, "'People do not live by bread alone, but by every word that comes from the mouth of God'" (Matthew 4:4). This was His response to Satan after fasting for forty days and nights. He was quoting a very familiar passage to the first-century Jewish ear, when Moses reminded the Israelites how God disciplined but also cared for them in the wilderness.

> Yes, he humbled you by letting you go hungry and then feeding you with manna, a food previously unknown to you and your ancestors. He did it to teach you that people do not live by

bread alone; rather, we live by every word that comes from the mouth of the Lord (Deuteronomy 8:3).

We live by every word that comes from the mouth of God. If we are going to survive in this broken world, much less thrive, it begins by feeding our souls with the very word of God.

Devouring the Bible can take many different forms. Of course, we read the Bible and study the Bible. Donald Whitney says the main difference between reading and studying is simply a pen and paper, but we'll dig in to this later on. Reading can happen out loud or silently. Reading and studying can happen in solitude or in community. We can hear the Bible—whether that's listening to someone else read scripture or hearing it read aloud and taught at church on Sunday morning or in a sermon podcast. We can meditate on scripture. We can memorize scripture. We can pray scripture. All of these are different ways to consume the Word of God. Think of it as different small plates at a tapas restaurant. It's all delicious, edible food—but each plate has a variety of ingredients, differing presentations, perhaps even certain dishes you prefer more than others. But it all serves the same purpose of delighting the palette, addressing hunger, and nourishing our bodies.

No More Shame in This Game

Every Christian knows they are *supposed* to read the Bible, but so many of us struggle to actually do it on a regular basis. If that's you, I want you to hear there is no *condemnation in Christ Jesus*,* which means there is absolutely no judgment or shaming coming from me. Remember the words of my mom: There is nothing you can do that will make God

---
* Romans 8:1

love you more, and there is nothing you can do that will make Him love you less.

Reading your Bible every day won't make God love you more. What it can do—if we do it with the right posture—is give you peace, hope, joy, wisdom, and all kinds of other resources to help you navigate this life. It will also deepen your knowledge of and love for God like nothing else can. Putting your face in the Bible on a regular basis has nothing to do with being a "good Christian"; it has everything to do with nourishing your soul and equipping you to live a life worthy of His calling.

In 2009, a study with 40,000 participants[3] made the astounding discovery that if a person read or listened to the Bible four times a week, they experienced a dramatic change in the following ways:

- Feeling lonely dropped 30 percent
- Anger issues dropped 32 percent
- Bitterness in relationships dropped 40 percent
- Alcoholism dropped 57 percent
- Sex outside of marriage dropped 68 percent
- Feeling spiritually stagnant dropped 60 percent
- Viewing pornography dropped 61 percent
- Sharing one's faith jumped 200 percent
- Discipling others jumped 230 percent

But this isn't that surprising, right? I mean, isn't this what God's Word promises us? What would have been truly shocking is if there had been no significant results for those who spent more than half of their week interacting with God's Word.

While we know ingesting scripture is vital to our health and wellness, many of us still struggle to find any kind of consistency. Whether it's the lack of time, energy, know-how, or resources, we just don't do it. This is where our science of habit formation is going to kick in beautifully. Our goal here is to create a habit of showing up. We're going to start small and cultivate a habit that makes Bible intake automatic in our daily lives.

Remember, automatic isn't bad. Most of our habits are automatic. When you walk up to the sink, you don't wonder, *Now how do I get water to come out again?* You just turn it on without thinking. When you get into your car, you don't need to consciously think through how to turn it on or buckle your seat belt. You just do it. When you walk into a dark room, again, you already know what to do. Your brain has been wired to quickly access the solution to these everyday moments. In the same way, we want our habits of Bible intake, prayer, thanksgiving, and more to be what we automatically do all day long.

A while back, I had a really hard night after a painful argument with someone close to me. Even after it ended, I couldn't settle down. I stayed up way too late as my mind raced and my emotions exploded into every corner of my body. My cortisol levels were through the roof, and I didn't know if I'd ever fall asleep.

When my alarm went off the next morning, my mind immediately jumped right back to where it was the night before—anxiety, turmoil, heartache—it all came rushing back. I was physically exhausted, but my heart compelled my body out of bed and into the wingback chair in my home office, where I opened the Bible. It was like a balm for my oozing wounds. Just as I automatically reach for a glass of water and ibuprofen when I have a headache, it was automatic for me to crawl to the scriptures to address my aching heart.

Even though I had a set reading plan to follow, I felt compelled to open to the pages of Psalm 139 and Ephesians 4. Slowly, meditatively, and prayerfully, I read the verses—some out loud, some silently. I let the words of God wash over me, as if the text were a pain-soothing, germ-fighting medicinal ointment for my breaking heart.

Did spending time in God's Word change my circumstances? I wish. Did it strengthen me, encourage me, guide me, and sustain me? Without a doubt. Did all of my anxieties and hurt melt away? Not exactly, but it helped me surrender them at His feet. It reminded me that He cares about my pain and that He will use this awful situation to deepen my dependence on Him and mature me spiritually. It gave me things to ponder, chew on, and prayerfully consider as I took stock of my own part in the situation. While I may not be in control of the circumstance, I am in control of my thoughts, attitude, and response. I need God's Word to show me where I'm wrong and how to think and behave. Ultimately, I need to be healed and transformed. But in order to receive that, I have to actively spend time in His presence and in His Word. There's no other way.

What's the Purpose: Transformation Over Information

The point of reading the Bible is not to learn more about the Bible. I cannot stress this enough. Gaining information about the Bible is usually a byproduct of time spent in the Word, but it is not the purpose of reading and study. We open the word of God; we ingest it; we sit in it; we bathe in it for the purpose of getting to know God. Full stop.

God, in His infinite kindness and desire to be in relationship with us, chose to reveal Himself to us, chose to teach us about who He is, who we are, and what His sovereign plans are through the inspired writings of prophets and apostles, which we now have bound by glue or stitch in paperback and hardback, and on those little handheld devices we so dearly love in at least sixty different English translations.

The purpose of reading or studying the Bible isn't to check off a box or to increase our scriptural knowledge. In fact, Jesus criticized the Pharisees for this very attitude, and in turn warns us:

> You search the Scriptures because you think they give you eternal life. But the Scriptures point to me! Yet you refuse to come to me to receive this life (John 5:39–40).

The Pharisees were experts in the Torah. By age twelve or thirteen, Jewish boys were expected to have memorized large chunks of the Law. It is widely believed that the Pharisees had memorized the entire first five books of the Old Testament, plus additional texts from the Prophets* and Wisdom Literature.** They knew God's Word better than anyone, but Jesus said they missed the meaning of it all. The scriptures point to Him! The purpose of knowing our Bible is so that we know Him. **We don't read for information; we read for transformation.**

There are many of us who already have a regular practice of reading, studying, or hearing the Bible—maybe you do it first thing in the morning or last thing before you go to sleep—but after you close your Bible, you kind of forget you ever opened it. You can't recall what you learned, and it doesn't seem to be having any kind of impact. If that's true for you, you might be reading for information—or out of obligation—instead of transformation.

Again, please believe me—there is no shame coming from me here! But if this is you, I want to bring awareness to your situation. Hang in there with me. We'll talk about how to transition from information to transformation soon.

---

* Books like Isaiah, Jeremiah, Lamentations, and Ezekiel.
** Wisdom literature includes Job, Psalms, Proverbs, and Ecclesiastes.

To paraphrase John Mark Comer, knowing what the Bible says is not the same as having the mind of Christ.[4] We want our neural pathways to be rewired to think like Jesus through a lifetime of chewing on scripture. If we accomplish the goal of reading through the Bible in a year—that's wonderful! But if we haven't become more loving, more patient, more kind, more gentle, more humble, more forgiving, more compassionate—more like Jesus—we missed the point. Spending time in the word of God should change us day by day. It should transform us into His likeness.

This is the beauty of creating Seed Habits for biblical consumption. We can create tiny but powerful habits, scattered throughout our day, that constantly bring us back to God and His Word.

I once read a journalist's account of Billy Graham's home, where Bibles were laid open in nearly every room throughout his house. When the journalist asked Billy what his devotional life looked like (and while Billy had a robust reading and studying practice), he simply pointed to the Bibles spread throughout the house.

His grandson, Roy, shared a story that explained how Billy moved around his open Bibles:

> He walked out of his bedroom one time, walked by an open Bible, read two or three lines real quick—within seconds—then walked on up to the kitchen. My grandmother and I were sitting there by the fire and I was adding more wood to it. He came back down, read a couple more sentences on the way back to his bedroom. And I asked him, "What could you have gotten out of that Bible in that short amount of time?" He turned around and looked at me and said, "I sip on the Word of God all day long." A smart aleck teenager was just handed it right back to him from his own grandfather.[5]

Sip, sip, sip. Billy was constantly sipping just a little bit of the Bible as he moved throughout his day. What a beautiful example of a Seed Habit.

The Bible is one* of God's chosen ways to reveal Himself to us. Over a span of two centuries, He revealed Himself to mankind and gave His words to forty human authors, who recorded those revelations over three different continents. Then, He made sure those records were kept, protected for centuries, and translated into several languages until eventually the Gutenberg press was invented—which really put God's Word into the hands of everyday people for the first time ever. Since then, the Bible has been translated into over 3,756 languages.**

So, if the Bible really is God's way of revealing Himself to us, then reading, studying, hearing, meditating on, and memorizing even the smallest portions of His Word is the absolute best thing we can feed our minds. Robert Morgan writes, "Bible verses represent the most healing, clarifying, bolstering, uplifting data we can insert into our brains. The power of Scripture is unlike anything else on earth. It's a force to be reckoned with, containing intrinsic power, high enough to give us insight, deep enough to give us peace, wide enough to mold our personalities, and strong enough to bear us through horrendous days."[6]

This is why we want to sip, snack, munch, and devour the Word of the Living God. We ingest it to grow: to grow in the likeness of Jesus, to grow in wisdom, to grow in love.

---

* I say one way because God has revealed Himself to us in the person of Jesus Christ, in creation (Romans 1:20, Psalm 19:1–4, Job 12:7–10), and through the Holy Spirit. Of course, the Bible may be the most concrete and thorough, considering it includes how we know Jesus Christ today.

** 3,756 languages is the total number with some portion of scripture. The Bible in its entirety has only been translated into 756 languages so far. The New Testament alone has been translated into an additional 1,726 languages, and then there are another 1,274 languages that have at least some portion of scripture. Amazingly, this means up to 98 percent of all people in the world have access to some amount of scripture in their native tongue.

Throughout his letters to the church, the Apostle Paul says we personally grow as we learn to know God better. We grow as we learn more about His infinite love for us. We mature in wisdom and insight as we deepen our knowledge of God.* Spending time in the word of God gives us access to learn more about who He is, which in turn transforms us into new creations that are more like Him.

Let's look at five ways we can experience and ingest God's Word on a regular basis: reading, studying, hearing, meditating, and memorizing.

Reading

"The Bible was written not to satisfy your curiosity but to help you conform to Christ's image."

—Howard Hendricks[7]

Remember the friend I mentioned in chapter two—the one who said she wouldn't open her Bible unless she had enough time to read a full chapter? This is exactly where we all need to shift our mindset from the "go big or go home" mentality to one that embraces the science of habit formation. As I said before, our goal is to create a habit of showing up to an open Bible. If you've never had a daily habit of opening and reading your Bible, it can feel incredibly intimidating to start. What do you read? How long do you read? How do you make it stick with you or have any kind of impact?

First, we have to begin with a plan and a place. Just like if you want a consistent, effective workout routine, you need a plan. If you show up to the gym and from there it's open-ended, you might hop on the treadmill for a bit, do some machines for your arms, and maybe look

---

* Ephesians 1:16–17, 3:18; Colossians 1:9–10

around the gym for some inspiration and copy someone else's moves, but if that's your long-term plan, it's not going to be very effective. On the days when you wake up and don't feel like going to the gym, it's going to be really easy to skip out if you don't have a plan in place that you know you're going to miss.

My favorite workout plans give me six workouts a week that change up every three or four weeks. Every day when I wake up, I know exactly what I need to accomplish in the gym. Not only does it help me make the most of my time, but it gives me a holistic workout plan. I also have a set place where I accomplish this plan. A few years ago, my husband and I decided to invest in a home gym setup, and we've loved it more than I ever could have imagined.

A PRAYER FOR BIBLE READING: Lord, please meet me here as I open your Word. Help me to understand it and apply it to my day. Reveal yourself to me. Guide me in your truth. As I sit in your Word, show me what you want to say to me right now.

In the same way, it's incredibly helpful for us to have a place and a plan for reading the Bible. It doesn't have to be fancy. Prior to becoming a mom, I had fairly consistent Bible reading and studying habits. I often utilized robust studies that required a lot of time each week. But after having two babies in eighteen months, I was dying for something incredibly simple. I wanted to be in my Bible regularly—in fact I was starving for it—but I didn't have it in me to commit to anything challenging or time-consuming. One day, I had the idea to just choose one book of the Bible to read and study for an entire month. So, for the month of October, I decided I was going to read the book of Philippians.

If you're familiar with Philippians, you probably know it's only four chapters. In fact, it only takes the average reader about ten to twelve minutes to read the entire book in one sitting. So, I figured if I gave myself thirty-one days to read something that should only take ten to twelve minutes, I'd probably be in good shape. Some days I read an entire chapter, and some days just a short section. Sometimes I just pondered one verse for a while. Every time I got through the book, I would simply start over and choose a new English translation to read it in. I worked on memorizing a few verses. But no matter what, I just tried to open my Bible once a day and read something out of the book of Philippians.

I had a plan; I made it small and easy (remember the first two rules in our Seed Habit formula?), and I made it fit by reading while I nursed my baby every morning. My "place" was the rocking chair. I could have made it easy by leaving an open Bible on the nightstand in my son's nursery, but I chose an even easier route by reading on my phone. In general, I avoid reading on my phone. I don't like it; I want to feel the physical Bible in my hand. I like to turn pages and see a bigger picture of the context that a phone screen doesn't allow. But at that time in my life, opening a Bible app and being able to easily navigate translations, or even press play and let someone else read it to me, was what I needed. It had to be as simple as possible so that I could cultivate a habit of showing up. So my Seed Habit was:

After I begin to nurse, I will pick up my phone and read Philippians.

Y ou need a plan and you need a place.

A few plan ideas to get you started:

Pick a book of the Bible to read through for a month.

Billy Graham read five psalms a day ("that teaches me how to get along with God"), a proverb a day ("that teaches me how to get along with my fellow man"), a gospel each week, and "constantly returned to Acts."[8] While it would be very "go big or go home" of you to do the Billy Graham plan, do you want to take a tiny piece of his plan and make it your own?

Search online for a 5 x 5 x 5 plan. These plans are five minutes a day, for five days a week, with five ways to dig deeper.

Do you need to read scripture about joy? Peace? Fighting anxiety? Hope? A quick internet search could point you to a book of the Bible that relates to your current circumstances.

If you want to create a Seed Habit for reading your Bible—whether it's the first time you've cultivated a daily reading habit or you want to add some additional reading into your day like Billy Graham—perhaps your Seed Habit is:

After I press start on the coffee maker, I will read my Bible until my coffee is ready.

Again, we need a plan here. So figure out what you're going to read for one minute.

As for your place, can you leave an open Bible in that spot? Maybe with a highlighter or pen? This is such a good way to start small and slowly let it grow. I truly believe if you start here, you'll find you start spending more and more time reading and studying your Bible in this one spot.

Or maybe your Seed Habit is:

After I begin brushing my teeth, I will read my Bible for two minutes. (And you can do this twice a day!)

Can you leave an open Bible next to your sink to remember to do this?

Studying

"No Spiritual Discipline is more important than the intake of God's Word. Nothing can substitute for it. There simply is no healthy Christian life apart from a diet of the milk and meat of Scripture."
—DONALD S. WHITNEY,
Spiritual Disciplines for the Christian Life[9]

Reading God's Word on a daily basis is like going to the Starbucks drive-through and being handed your coffee. You can savor that cup of coffee and absolutely love it. It gives you the caffeine you need. It tastes delightful. And you could drink coffee that way your entire life and be fine.

Studying God's Word is like buying raw beans, taking them home, and roasting them. Then learning to grind, measure, and make your own pour-over coffee every morning. It takes a lot more time, effort, and resources, but you will learn so much more about coffee, your palette will be heightened, and you'll actually enjoy it even more.

Or so I'm told. This is coming from a girl who buys her beans from Costco. So, if you prefer gas station coffee to pour-over, that's just fine with me. I am not here to judge your coffee choices. But if you already have a regular routine of reading God's Word, maybe it's time to start a Seed Habit of studying.

Studying the Bible can start very simply with a pen and paper. You write down things you observe or notice in the text. You write down questions you have about the text. You use the cross-references in your Bible to look up other pages and see how that expands your understanding of the passage. Then, you find an online concordance to look up certain words and see how they're used in other passages. You gather a commentary or two to reference as you go.* You read different English translations and note the differences that bring insight—or perhaps more questions.

The beautiful thing about studying the Bible is that it is truly exhaustive. You can never out-dig or out-study the Bible, and whether you dig with a spoon or an excavator, you're going to uncover new things. So it's okay to begin with a spoon and just do a little at a time. You have a lifetime of cultivating this habit and letting it grow. You'll slowly find more resources and commentaries to aid you on your way. You can even join a Bible study where people gather to seriously study and share their findings and insights on scripture. But don't feel like you need to start studying with all the resources for an hour a day. Remember to start small.

Maybe your Seed Habit is simply to begin your Bible reading time with a pen and paper. That's it. You write down a few observations and a question each day. It's small, it's easy, it fits, and you can slowly let

---

* I love practically everything from BibleProject, and I am a huge fan of Tom Constable's "Notes."

it grow. If you want more guidance on how to study the Bible, flip to Appendix B!

Hearing

"I think there's tremendous value in hearing God's word read out loud simply because for many generations it was the only way people heard it. They heard it read in the home or in church or in public spaces. There were so many generations during which people just could not read, and so it was always an audible thing. There's something very powerful about Scripture being read."

—KRISTYN GETTY[10]

Until about the mid-1400s, most people only experienced the Bible by hearing it read aloud. While we should absolutely take advantage of our access to scripture in written form, I think it's worth remembering that listening to the Bible is also a beautiful way to ingest it. Remember the study mentioned earlier about the effects of Bible intake at least four days a week? Its findings showed that reading and listening had the same effect. In Isaiah 55:11, God says through the mouth of Isaiah:

> So is my word that goes out from my mouth: It will not return to me empty, but will accomplish what I desire and achieve the purpose for which I sent it (NIV).

The Bible is the word out of God's mouth. It doesn't matter if it's read or heard, it will not return void. It will accomplish His will—which for our purposes means it will impact and transform us.

I know folks who listen to large chunks of scripture every day. They love it, retain it, and reap the benefits. I, on the other hand, have a very hard time staying focused and attuned to scripture being read to me. I much prefer to see it and read it myself. However, I have begun the practice of reading scripture out loud during my own private time of reading. I recently heard Beth Moore quote a poet—it may have been W. B. Yeats—with the sentiment that poetry demands to be read aloud. So whenever she comes to a prayer or some poetry in scripture, she always reads it aloud. Now I do too.

Meditating

"Sometimes His word makes such an impact on me that I have to put the Bible down and walk around for a few moments to catch my breath."

—BILLY GRAHAM[11]

Since we used coffee for our reading and studying analogy, tea makes the perfect illustration for meditating. When we meditate, our mind is the hot water and the tea bag is God's Word. We can dunk it in and out, over and over, throughout the day. We can let it simply sit and permeate the water. The longer we leave the tea bag in the water, the more the water will transform into the likeness of the tea.

In the Old Testament, there are two different Hebrew words that encompass meditation. We see them translated in English as listening to God's Word, ruminating on God's law, remembering God's deeds, and more. When we add them all up, we read this concept of meditation fifty-eight times in the Old Testament alone.

In the New Testament we find encouragements like:

Let the word of Christ dwell in you richly . . . (Colossians 3:16, ESV)

Reflect on what I'm saying . . . (2 Timothy 2:7, NIV)

Look carefully into the perfect law that sets you free . . . (James 1:25)

Dwell on these things . . . (Philippians 4:8, CSB)

Fix your thoughts on Jesus . . . (Hebrews 3:1, NIV)

In Psalm 1, King David paints a picture of the benefits of meditating on God's Word:

But his delight is in the law of the LORD, and on his law he meditates day and night. He is like a tree planted by streams of water that yields its fruit in its season, and its leaf does not wither. In all that he does, he prospers (Psalm 1:2–3, ESV).

When we meditate on God's truth and it becomes so engrained into who we are, we become a sturdy oak tree who is steadfast, fruitful, protected from surrounding elements, and prosperous. And while this is about to seem too good to be true, I think meditation may be the simplest Seed Habit anyone can implement. You can use meditation in the most mundane elements of your day to radically change your perspective and invite God's Spirit to transform you as you run errands, do laundry, sit in meetings, prepare dinner, and answer late-night emails.

It's as simple as picking one word, phrase, or verse to meditate on throughout your day. Sometimes I choose a new verse each day from whatever I read that morning. This is the best way I know to fight against the unwanted consequence of reading your Bible, closing it, and never thinking about it until you open it up tomorrow. But many times I hold on to one verse for several weeks. At the time of writing this, my meditation verse is Ephesians 4:2:

> Always be humble and gentle. Be patient with each other, making allowance for each other's faults because of your love.

I rehearse this verse over and over in my head all day long and watch as it transforms my relationships.

Now, meditation cannot really be done without memorization. If we are just meditating on one word or phrase, it may be a very light version of memorization, but in general the two are very closely linked.

Memorizing

"While Scripture reading and study are daily disciplines I will hold on to for life, memorization has been a bridge between reading and living."

—GLENNA MARSHALL[12]

In his book *100 Bible Verses Everyone Should Know by Heart,** Robert Morgan makes the observation that:

> We are what we think, and our lives run in the direction of our thoughts. If we think angry thoughts, we'll be angry; if we think positive thoughts, we'll be positive; if we think negative

---

* Which I highly recommend if this is a Seed Habit you want to begin or take to the next level.

thoughts, we'll be negative. The mind is a garden, and we have to cultivate it, and we are responsible for the kind of seed we sow into the furrows of our mind.

—ROBERT MORGAN[13]

Memorizing scripture is a way to be intentional about the seed we sow. Instead of just ruminating on positivity and gratitude (both of which I'm a fan of), we can be filling our minds with—as Robert Morgan says—"the best thoughts ever recorded."[14] Since the Bible is the very Word of God, why wouldn't we want to deeply plant it into our subconscious through memorization?

Glenna Marshall's book *Memorizing Scripture** opens with the statement "There are few disciplines Christians want to do more but actually do less than memorizing Scripture."[15] Just like reading our Bibles, we all know this is something we would greatly benefit from, but most of us haven't memorized a Bible verse since childhood. I wonder if we don't memorize scripture because it seems overwhelming. There are 31,102 verses from Genesis to Revelation.** We'll never memorize all of that, so what could one hundred verses*** really do for us? To once again lean on Robert Morgan's words:

When we memorize a word, phrase, line, or verse from God's Word, it's like implanting a powerful radioactive speck of the very mind of God into our own finite brains.[16]

---

* Another resource I highly recommend.

** This number is from the Protestant Bible, but of course it would vary if you picked up a Catholic or Orthodox Bible.

*** In case you're wondering—which I was—that's 0.0032 percent of the Bible. That sure doesn't seem like a drop in the bucket, does it?

Memorizing and meditating on scripture is perhaps the best tool we have in changing our thought life. At the beginning of my seminary program, I had to fill out a lengthy and personal spiritual assessment. One section required me to identify and write out a list of any negative thought patterns I held on to. Then, I had to find scripture that would combat those thoughts. One of the consistent negative thought patterns I struggled with was negative thoughts about my own kids. I hesitated to even include this, knowing how sensitive and easily misunderstood this could be, but I also know I'm not the only mom out there who gets hit with thoughts like these. So, let me be clear: I love my kids fiercely. I adore them. They are the delight of my life, and I would die for them. I'd do anything to protect them. But for whatever reason—call it sin, spiritual warfare, the effects of stress, whatever—I still had this tape playing in my head with negative thoughts that I truly didn't mean or believe. So, at the encouragement of this assessment, I wrote down a couple phrases from Psalm 127:3–5:

Children are a blessing from the Lord. Children are a reward.

Later that day, I walked into my bathroom and saw my new package of floss opened and completely unraveled with minty-fresh, white string filling my entire vanity like Spidey was there to save the day. I took a deep breath and screamed inside my head: *CHILDREN ARE A BLESSING FROM THE LORD.*

Then when I found a large block of high-quality and expensive parmesan cheese stashed in the corner of our living room, gnawed on by what looked like a rat but was certainly my two-year-old, I internally yelled, *CHILDREN ARE A REWARD!*

Later, when I found Sharpie scribbled all over the entry hallway walls, I again internally shouted, *CHILDREN ARE A BLESSING! THANK YOU, GOD, FOR MY BLESSINGS.*

And then there was the day I walked into the kitchen to find a strange light pink substance scattered and pulverized all over our wood floor—as far as the eye could see—only to realize my three blessings had dumped a pound of deli ham on the ground and proceeded to roll over it, back and forth, back and forth, with their scooters (which they are not allowed to ride in the house). I yelled externally: "WHAT IN THE ACTUAL HELL?!"

Okay, so it didn't work every time. But three out of four ain't bad. And in all seriousness, I now no longer think those negative thoughts at all. It's been years since those horrible thoughts came to my mind. Do they still do asinine things? You better believe it. Do I still get angry, want to scream, actually scream, pull out my hair, and more? Sure do! But the word of God truly uprooted those negative thoughts, and many times I am able to shake my head and laugh at whatever absurd mess they've made (while still dreaming up the best, most memorable consequence for the destruction they caused). I really do believe that children are a blessing from the Lord. I always did, but thanks to the habits of meditation and memorization, I was able to uproot my negative thoughts and replace them with God's thoughts.

We begin small with memorization by choosing one verse at a time—even short verses! Don't overcomplicate it. Set yourself up for success. If you've never practiced memorization before, don't set your goal to memorize all of Romans 1 or Psalm 119. (Don't go big!) Pick a verse that meets you where you are. If you're struggling with anxiety, find a verse about peace. If you're struggling with anger, find a verse about patience or forgiveness. If you're struggling with fear, find a verse about trusting God.

Then, when it's time to let it grow, push yourself just a bit. Can you memorize two verses a month? Four? Can you start working on a chunk of verses? Can you eventually grow that into an even larger section?

Once Again, It's Okay
(and Actually Vital!) to Start Small

At the risk of sounding like a broken record, this entire book is about starting small. It may feel like one Bible verse or one minute isn't enough, but our goal with Seed Habits is to cultivate the habit of showing up. If you have never eaten three big meals a day, you probably don't have the appetite for that. So, we begin by growing our appetite in small, sustainable ways. You eat small meals, a snack or two. Then that grows into more snacks, a larger meal, and another, and another. Eventually, we're eating twelve thousand calories a day like we're Michael Phelps. Or, to put it like Billy Graham: We find ways to sip, sip, and sip the very word of God throughout our day.

Remember the drill? Make it small. Make it easy. Make it fit. Let it grow.

Seed Habits

I've given you a lot of information on the ways we devour the Bible, but if this is the place you want to begin cultivating one to three Seed Habits, here are some ideas to jump-start your thinking.

Reading Scripture:
- After I start the coffee maker, I will read my (already open) Bible (because I left it there on purpose) while my coffee brews.

- After I begin brushing my teeth, I will read my Bible for two minutes. (And you can do this twice a day!)
- After I sit down to eat breakfast, I will read one Bible chapter.
- After I get in bed, I will read a short section (just a few verses!) of scripture before turning off the light.

Studying Scripture:

- After I finish my daily reading, I will spend two minutes jotting down any observations or questions I have.
- After I finish my daily reading, I will spend two minutes reading a commentary (look up Tom Constable's "Notes"!) on the passage I just read.
- When I finish my Bible reading, I will look up one cross-reference from the passage and jot down a note about the connection.
- On Saturday mornings, instead of my normal habit of reading, I will spend my time studying a passage I already read this week.

Hearing Scripture:

- After I get in the car each morning, I will listen to one minute of scripture.*
- After I begin walking the dog, I will listen to two minutes of scripture.
- After I finish my workout, I will listen to one minute of scripture while I transition to whatever I'm doing next.

---

* There are several great apps to help you do this, like The Bible App by Life.Church or Dwell: Audio Bible. There are also a number of podcasts that read a chapter a day in dozens of different translations. There are even podcasts for listening to the Bible while you fall asleep.

Or if you want to begin reading out loud during your daily reading time:

- After I open my Bible, I will read my day's passage aloud or cue up the same passage in a Bible app and listen to it while I read along.
- After I come across a prayer or poem in scripture, I will read it out loud.

Meditating on Scripture:
- After I read my Bible, I will pick out one phrase to meditate on for the day. I will write it on a sticky note, on my hand, or set it on my phone lock screen so that I see it frequently throughout the day.
- I will prayerfully pick a verse to meditate on all month. After I flush the toilet or while I wash my hands, open the fridge, or load the dishwasher (just choose one prompt!), I will meditate on that verse.
- After I lose my temper or feel anxious or afraid (or some unwanted cycle you're in), I will meditate on a verse that can transform my mind. NOTE: This is a harder cue because we don't lose our temper at the same time each day.* But it's a great way to begin implementing Seed Habits at a "pro" level. You can identify unwanted habits and turn those into cues that will remind you to do your wanted Seed Habit.
- After I turn on the bath for my child, I will meditate on my weekly verse. I will tell my child about it too.

---

* Well, unless you have tiny people in your home who abide by the witching hour, and then you just might lose your temper every day at 5:00 p.m.

Memorizing Scripture:
- After I turn on the faucet to wash my hands, I will work on my Bible memory verse.
- After I walk into the gym, I will work on my Bible memory verse for thirty seconds. Or after I finish each set (at the gym), I will recite my Bible memory verse one time.
- After I pull into the carpool pick-up line, I will grab my Bible memory verse notecard and spend two minutes on it.
- After I stop at a red light, I will think on my Bible memory verse.

For all Bible memory Seed Habits, I highly recommend writing your verse down on a notecard you carry with you—or writing it down on several cards that you leave throughout your spaces (bathroom, car, gym bag, desk) or putting it on your phone lock screen. But I *strongly prefer* the notecard.

There are endless ways to incorporate small, easy moments of biblical intake into your everyday life. You just have to find what works for you!

Chapter Review

- Devouring the Bible includes all kinds of ways we interact with and ingest the Word of God, including reading, studying, hearing, meditating, and memorizing.
- Even these can be expressed differently by being done in solitude or with community.
- The purpose of feasting on God's Word is to be transformed. (Transformation over information!)

- If we're reading or studying the Bible but never remembering anything or seeing transformation, we may be reading to check off a box or simply to gain information.
- The more we spend time in God's Word, the more we should exude attributes of Him: peace, joy, patience, gentleness, compassion, forgiveness—and above all, love.
- To be successful with a consistent Bible-reading habit, you must have a plan and a place.

Homework

Jot down a few Seed Habits you may want to integrate into your day. These can just be rough ideas. You may decide to keep reading more chapters and choose different habits to begin with. But since you're here now, go ahead and write a few Devouring the Bible Seed Habits you may want to try.

Here are some basic ideas to get your wheels turning:

Read the Bible for one minute every day.

Read ten verses a day.

Read a Psalm or Proverbs each day.

Study for two minutes a day.

If you already read most days, set aside one day a week when you replace your reading time with studying. Study something you already read that week.

Listen to the Bible for two minutes a day.

Read the Bible out loud during your own time of reading/study.

Do it with a friend: Send a voice memo to a friend every day in which you read one Bible verse out loud. (Take turns.) Or do a group text with five friends, and each of you takes one day a week.

Choose one Bible verse, phrase, or word to meditate on.

Choose one Bible verse to memorize.

Now take those Seed Habits and put them in our formula (referencing your homework from chapter one to help you!).

After I _____, I will _____.

I gave you several ideas in the Seed Habit section—feel free to steal those!

Another key part of this process is to match your Seed Habit with a cue that occurs as often as you want to practice your habit. How many times do you want to sip, sip, sip?

Make It Stick

A few reminders from chapter two:

- Don't forget your habit will be stickier if you try the 7x method.

- Also remember the benefit of "celebrating" when you are newly practicing your habit.
- Finally, there is strength in numbers. Get a friend to do this with you. Pick three Seed Habits you both want to work on together and share the journey.

CHAPTER FOUR

Devoted to Prayer

"Of all spiritual disciplines prayer is the most central because it ushers us into perpetual communion with the Father."

—RICHARD J. FOSTER[1]

MY SON PAX WAS GIFTED A MOTORIZED ROCKET FOR HIS FIFTH BIRTH-day. You set the rocket on a tripod stand in an open area and press a button. The rocket launches about two hundred feet into the air, and (hopefully) the built-in parachute releases, allowing it to grace-fully land. The parachute works about half the time, but somehow this beloved rocket has remained intact and working for over a year.* One summer day, my boys thought it would be a good idea to launch the rocket in our backyard. Now, if you could see my backyard, you would know this is a terrible idea. Our house is on a quarter acre, so you could throw a rock and hit at least five neighboring houses. The boys launched the rocket, which sailed far and wide until it plummeted back down to

---

* Toy years are like dog years. So if a toy has lasted one year, that's really seven years in the toy time and space continuum.

the third-story roof of our neighbors' house. Needless to say, there was no ladder or human who would be willing to rescue the rocket. The boys were devastated.

"Mom, what are we going to do?"

"Well, boys," I chuckled, "the only thing that's going to get that rocket off that roof is a mighty gust of wind. Why don't you pray and ask God to send some wind to knock it off the roof? But it's going to have to be strong, because it will need to go from the third-story roof, clear the second-story roof, which is much wider, and then fall down from there onto their porch, and then we're going to have to awkwardly explain to our backyard neighbors—who we rarely speak to—that your rocket is on their porch. But go ahead and pray because I know God hears the prayers of His children, and He might just say yes to your request."

Isaac, my seven-year-old lawyer-in-training, responded, "Well, Mom, I don't know if that's a good prayer because what if God sends a tornado that destroys our neighborhood? That wouldn't be good."

"Good point. I guess you better be specific with your prayer."

So Pax prayed first, then Isaac, and they asked me to close it out.

"Okay, boys, let's wait and see. Watch expectantly."

We stood there quietly for about ten seconds,* watching and waiting.

"In my experience, God usually takes some time before answering prayers, so let's give it a bit, but keep your eyes open!"

Lord, I really hope you come through on this one, I silently prayed. *I know it'll be a lesson in prayer either way, but it'd be nice if you answered yes. Please show them you hear their prayers.*

---

* Similar to toy years, the amount of time a five- and a seven-year-old boy spend silent and still is multiplied by one hundred. So while it was only ten seconds, it was really one thousand seconds in boy time.

A few hours later, we were basking in the sun, swimming at our neighborhood pool, when out of nowhere—and I mean nowhere—the craziest gust of wind came rushing through the trees. It lasted for just a few seconds, but it was wild.

"What on earth was that?" my neighbor asked.

Me, grinning from ear to ear: "That, my friend, was God answering the prayers of two little boys who asked for their rocket back."

When we got home, the boys sprinted to our backyard to see if they could locate their little rocket. Not only had it fallen from the tippy-top of our neighbor's house, it had flown so far that it landed in our very own backyard.

Don't tell me God doesn't have a sense of humor.

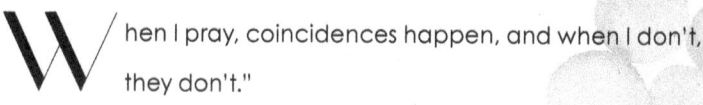

When I pray, coincidences happen, and when I don't, they don't."

—ARCHBISHOP WILLIAM TEMPLE[2]

Not unlike that wind, prayer is a wild thing. Throughout scripture we see prayers recorded in the Bible that changed the history of the world. In Numbers 14, we have a story where God changed His mind due to the intercession of Moses. In Philippians, while in prison, the Apostle Paul writes that he is confident he'll be delivered through the prayers of his fellow brothers and sisters in Christ and the provision of the Holy Spirit.*

---

* Philippians 1:19

Think about that for a moment. Paul, who had a radical encounter with Jesus on the road to Damascus, believed he would be delivered from prison not just by the power of the Holy Spirit, but also through—and notably, first mentioned—the prayers of God's people. Your prayers matter.

Matthew 6:8 tells us that God already knows what we need before we ask Him. So why did He create the experience of prayer? He doesn't need us to pray. Instead, it is an invitation for us to enter into His presence and be in relationship and communication with Him.

Wayne Grudem, one of my favorite theologians, said this:

Although God could care for all our needs in response to direct observation (Matthew 6:8), yet it has pleased God, in his relationship to the human race, to decide to act instead in response to prayer, apparently so that the faith shown through prayer might glorify him.[3]

Our prayers please God, they glorify God, because the act of praying requires faith. Hebrews 11:6 says without faith it's impossible to please God. We could be sinless, obey perfectly, and give all our money and possessions to the poor, but without faith in the Triune God, we cannot please Him. Prayer is one way we actively show—and grow—our faith.

So What Is Prayer?

In its simplest form, prayer is communication with God, but it goes much deeper than that. Prayer is an invitation to be in His presence. Prayer is faith in practice. Prayer is entrusting God with all the things that worry us about this life, knowing He is in control and we are not. Sometimes prayer is coming before the Lord and shutting up! Prayer is listening. It's sitting before the throne of God and allowing the Holy Spirit to guide you and minister to you. Prayer is so simple a child can do it, yet so multifaceted we'll never exhaust it or master it in our lifetime.

The first mention of prayer in the Bible happens in Genesis 4:26: "Seth* also had a son, and he named him Enosh. At that time people began to call on the name of the Lord." When we pray, we are calling on the name of the Lord. We are calling on God and asking Him to hear us and respond. Hebrews 4:16 says, "So let us come boldly to the throne of our gracious God. There we will receive his mercy, and we will find grace to help us when we need it most." God has granted us access to approach Him while He sits on His throne in ultimate power and authority.

You may know the story of Queen Esther, who decided to put her life on the line for her people, the Jews, as they faced a planned genocide. She risked her life because even as the queen, she was not permitted to simply approach the king on his throne. She had to be summoned. Any person who approached the king without being summoned by him risked the penalty of death.

This is why it was absolutely radical that the author of Hebrews told his original audience they could approach God's throne with boldness. You couldn't initiate approaching an earthly king, but the Ultimate King and Supreme Ruler of the entire Universe has given us an open-door policy through His Son, Jesus. And we don't even have to approach timidly or cautiously. We can be bold!

In the New Testament, the word "pray" and its derivatives appear 2,665 times! To say that prayer is a vital part of the Christian walk is the understatement of the century. Not only is it discussed, modeled, and

---

* Seth is the third-born son of Adam and Eve. He is born after their firstborn, Cain, kills their second-born, Abel. Basically, after the fall, things got messy fast.

consistently taught throughout scripture, there is also an emphasis on being devoted to prayer, being faithful in prayer, and praying without ceasing.

> Devote yourselves to prayer, being watchful in it with thanksgiving (Colossians 4:2, LSB)
> Pray without ceasing! (1 Thessalonians 5:17, ESV)
> Be joyful in hope, patient in affliction, faithful in prayer (Romans 12:12, NIV).

What Could It Look Like in Your Life to Be Devoted in Prayer or Pray Without Ceasing?

The Greek word translated as "without ceasing" in 1 Thessalonians was often used by Greek writers of the day to describe a hacking cough. So, "without ceasing" doesn't mean literally without stopping. We don't cough nonstop when we have a bad cold, but we do cough compulsively, constantly, and persistently. It often feels like you can't not cough. It almost controls you. So, to pray without ceasing is to live in such a way that you can't not pray. It's so automatic, so pervasive. You have such an attitude and posture of prayer throughout your day that you keep coming back to God in prayer.

To be devoted to prayer means to be devoted to Him. It means constant and continual dependence on Him. Devoted prayer sounds like brutal honesty with God. There is no need for pretense, no purpose in acting like you have it all together or you're not angry or disappointed. A devoted prayer life is coming as you are, all the time, into His presence. In Matthew 11, Jesus calls the weary and heavy-laden to Him. He doesn't say, "Come to me all you who have it together. Who have neither fear nor worries . . ." He invites us just as we are—tired, exhausted, burdened, overwhelmed—and His invitation to you is a life of connection to Him through prayer.

What Does It Look Like to Be Watchful in Prayer?

If you have kids, chances are one of those adorable creatures has gotten hold of a permanent marker or crayon and proudly scribbled all over your white sofa, their bedroom wall, or some other very much unwanted spot. All three of my children have done their fair share of "decorating." Not too long ago, I was down on my knees, relentlessly scrubbing a wall in an attempt to remove my burgeoning Picasso's hot pink Sharpie art. If you've had the pleasure of using a Mr. Clean Magic Eraser, you may be familiar with the addictive feeling it gives you. Once I eliminated the pink Sharpie (and some of the wall paint for that matter), I began noticing other marks and scuffs that I quickly went to work on. Soon I had moved from one wall to another, and another. It's as if holding the Magic Eraser opens your eyes to see your home in a way you've never seen it before! All of these unwanted marks on my walls that I currently have the power to wipe clean. (Why am I suddenly feeling drunk with power? Ah, the influence of that bald, one-earringed man.)

As I was vigorously, magically erasing, Colossians 4:2 came to mind.* *Devote yourselves to prayer, being watchful in it* . . . Before the pink Sharpie art, I hadn't noticed the dozens of other marks. But the latest toddler decoration forced me to get on my knees and look at my wall from a new perspective. After spending time solely focused on her hot pink designs, I became watchful. My eyes were opened to another mark, and then another. I think this is half the meaning of being watchful in prayer. The more we devote ourselves to it, the more our eyes will be open to all of the other things we can bring to the throne room of

---

* Full disclosure: I was actively memorizing that verse during this time. So it wasn't a totally random epiphany!

God. The tool in our hand is no longer a three-by-five block of white foam, it's the habit of entering the presence of God with anything and everything we need to bring before Him.

I also think being *watchful in it* is exactly what I told my boys when they prayed for a gust of wind to bring their rocket home. We pray expectantly, knowing God hears us and will answer. He may not always answer the way we want Him to, but He always answers. Even silence that means "wait" is an answer.

Prayer in the Bible

Scripture records over 650 prayers in the Bible. That blows my mind. Six hundred and fifty prayers of saints and sinners were written down over centuries for us to have, hold, and read. Twenty-five of those prayers were uttered by Jesus Himself. When I first learned this, it stopped me in my tracks. If you had asked me how many of Christ's prayers were recorded, I would have guessed five or six. WRONG. The prayers of Jesus add up quickly because He is constantly praying one sentence here or there amidst His teaching and public ministry. Not only are twenty-five prayers recorded, but the gospel tells us many more times that Jesus was praying, prayed, or taught about prayer.

The disciples saw this modeled day in and day out, and something about the way Jesus prayed—the frequency, the authority, the intimacy—compelled them to specifically ask him to teach them to pray. I take great solace in this. Perhaps the main reason we are not good at praying is because it's challenging. It's hard to live an ordinary day with supernatural eyes. It's difficult to remember God is always near, waiting to listen. It's tough to cultivate a habit of talking to God instead of picking up the phone to call a friend. It requires faith—real faith—to pray to an invisible God about all of our anxieties and fears. Even those who were closest to Jesus when He walked this earth, those who traveled with Him, heard all of His teachings, ate with Him, reclined with Him, watched Him minister and perform miracles, listened to and watched Him pray—even they felt like they just didn't quite get it. They needed their Master to teach them to pray.

In response to His disciples' request, Jesus gave them a model or sample prayer in what we call "The Lord's Prayer."* The prayer has two parts—the first focuses on God:

> *Our Father in heaven,*
> *may your name be kept holy.*
> *May your Kingdom come soon.*
> *May your will be done on earth,*
> *as it is in heaven.*
> *(Matthew 6:9–10)*

Jesus is teaching His disciples to relate to God as their Heavenly, Holy Father. He is reminding them to look up at the One who is in control of all things and to remember it's all His. As His children, we are invited to be part of these things—keeping His name holy (glorifying Him, testifying of His goodness, living in such a way that reflects His holiness), and actively participating in doing His will on earth.

Then, Jesus switches to a prayer that focuses on our everyday needs:

> *Give us today the food we need,*
> *and forgive us our sins,*
> *as we have forgiven those who sin against us.*
> *And don't let us yield to temptation,*
> *but rescue us from the evil one.*
> *(Matthew 6:11–13)*

---

* My dad has often said a better title would be "The Disciples' Prayer."

We ask God to provide for our literal human needs. We ask God to provide for our spiritual need of forgiveness, with the reminder that we must forgive others. And finally, we ask for His strength to endure the trials and tribulations of this world, so that we may be His will on earth.

The prayer invites us to daily trust God, to love and forgive one another, and to participate in God's will on earth.[4] While you can certainly pray this prayer word for word and join the saints of past and present around the globe, this prayer wasn't meant to be the only words we utter, but rather a guide. When we look at this prayer we see:

- Praise and adoration (or worship)
- Confession of sin
- Petitions for our needs, but don't miss that the pronouns are plural! *Give us.* This prayer models praying for self and others.
- Forgiveness of others*
- Protection from the enemy and spiritual forces at work in our world
- And while it is not modeled overtly in this prayer, thanksgiving is an underlying element. Since Paul mentions thanksgiving almost fifty times, I think it's safe to say it should be incorporated into our prayers.

These are the basic elements of a diverse prayer life.** As you grow in your prayer life, as you begin to seek the Kingdom of God throughout

---

* In my opinion this is the most frequently missed element of prayer. It is so important to Christ that we love and forgive others fully that He highlighted it in this very short prayer. When was the last time you sat before the Lord and asked him about unforgiveness in your heart? Who do you need to forgive? What hurts do you need to let go of? Forgiveness is the hallmark of Christianity. If we are not regularly forgiving others, we are not living as true followers of Jesus.

** I have a free, printable download that summarizes this, if you'd like a small, easy guide to help you in your practice of prayer. You can find it at www.hannaseymour.com/ESH.

your ordinary day, consider weaving these different focuses of prayer throughout your day.

However, we must remember that prayer is learned through practice. We grow in our ability and frequency of prayer as we do it.

But What About Those "Unanswered Prayers"?

We all have them. I have prayers I have boldly, angrily, timidly, exhaustedly, joyfully, annoyingly, grievingly brought to God for over a decade. The same prayers. Prayers He has not fully answered, or at least not in the way I am asking Him to. I have diligently prayed, even fasted, during certain seasons for those prayers. I've committed to praying for a certain amount of time, on my knees, at a certain time of day, for a certain period of days. I have grown weary and said, "Lord, I can't pray about this anymore. Take it. It's Yours." And after some time passes, I get reinspired by a sermon or a prompting, and I take up the mantle again to "storm the gates of heaven," as my grandmare used to say. I'm still waiting. I may wait my entire earthly life to see the answers to some of my prayers.

Perhaps my favorite Bible passage on prayer* is one so subtle that you may have never noticed it before. In the first chapter of his gospel account, Luke sets the scene for the long-awaited Jesus. His story begins with a priest named Zacharias and his wife, Elizabeth. Luke describes them as righteous and holy. They walked blameless before God, but they had no children. They had struggled with infertility their entire marriage, and now they were old. Based on the text, it's a fair assumption that Elizabeth was well beyond menopause. They had prayed for decades that God would open Elizabeth's womb, that God would bless them with a child, but God had not answered with a yes. During this

---

* I squirm even writing that because there are so many passages I am downright obsessed with when it comes to prayer.

time, infertility was viewed as a curse. It was believed that God was displeased with you; you were not righteous enough. Yet, Luke goes out of his way to let us know this was not the case for Zacharias and Elizabeth. God was very pleased with them, and yet in His perfect plan, it pleased Him to not give them a child during the years they begged Him for one.

This feels counterintuitive for us. Why would a good God not give us a good thing? Søren Kierkegaard eloquently said, "This is our comfort, because God answers every prayer; for either he gives what we pray for or something far better."[5]

In an article on singleness for those who might wish to be married, Paige Brown wrote, "It is a cosmic impossibility for God to shortchange any of his children."[6] Psalm 84:11 promises us that the Lord withholds no good thing from those who do what is right. That means that if you are praying for something that is good but God is withholding it, it's not good for you right now. The job promotion, the spouse, healing, a changed circumstance, a child—all good things, but God in His infinite wisdom knows what is best for you at this exact point in time, and you and I must decide if we trust Him to be the giver of good things, or a god who withholds them.

As for Zacharias and Elizabeth—I would imagine that after years of relentless prayer, you tire. (I know I have.) And once your childbearing years are truly, physically behind you, of course you stop praying about it. God has obviously said no, or maybe you wonder if He never heard you in the first place. Either way, you're past your prime, childless, and you decide you'll learn to be grateful for the life He has given you instead.

But then one day, when Zacharias is in the Holy of Holies interceding and offering sacrifices for God's people—a ritual he may have only been selected for once in his lifetime—an angel appears to him and says, "Do not be afraid, Zacharias, for your petition has been heard, and your wife Elizabeth will bear you a son . . ." (Luke 1:13, NASB 1995).

All of those years, you prayed and prayed asking God for a child, and you were met with silence? You were heard. All those times you begged, cried, pleaded with the Lord? He saw you. Even after you stopped petitioning God for a baby because you were advanced in years, and who in their right mind would keep praying for that? God did not forget you. Your petition has been heard.

The king and psalmist David wrote, "I love the LORD, because he has heard my voice and my pleas for mercy. Because he inclined his ear to me, therefore I will call on him as long as I live" (Psalm 116:1–2, ESV). He hears you. The God of the Universe hears you. Could that be enough reason to devote yourself to prayer? The simple fact that the Maker of Heaven and Earth listens to you? Another translation reads, "Because he bends down to listen, I will pray as long as I have breath!" (Psalm 116:2, NIV). What an image! The most powerful, eternal Being, Ruler of all, bends down to hear your whispered prayers.

> The important thing is to be honest to God, until He Himself gives the explanation which, whether it is the one you want or not, is always the best."
>
> —SØREN KIERKEGAARD[7]

Certainly there are times when God answers quickly. Sometimes He delivers the rocket only a few hours later. Sometimes the mass in your breast completely disappears two weeks later. Sometimes, after frantically searching for your debit card for days, you finally give up and utter a last-ditch prayer: "Lord, you know where my debit card is. Show me. I give up." Then, just ten minutes later, you find it. But many times, perhaps a majority of the time, our prayers last for months, years, even decades.

Jesus taught two parables on prayer that have a persistent asker—a persistent widow and a persistent neighbor. The point of these parables is not *if you nag God enough, He'll answer your prayer*, but rather *if evil men will finally give in to one who persists, your Good and Loving Father will, of course, answer your prayers.* Too often we think that the results of prayer are based upon our own determination. If I pray with enough passion, consistency, and fervor, surely God will answer. **But prayer is not about your determination—it's about your dependence on God.**

We serve a God who cares about your problem, yet it is your very problem that He uses to invite you into His presence. He can fix your problems—no problem! But more importantly, He'd rather you constantly be in His presence. God allows hardships; He even gives us trials as an opportunity to seek Him as our refuge and source of strength. We get to exchange our problems for His presence.

While prayers for our needs and wants (or others' needs and wants) may be what most often drive us to God's throne in the beginner stages of prayer, the simple act of constantly conversing with God will always reap wider benefits. When we train ourselves to constantly and continually go back to God, He aligns our hearts, desires, and perspectives with His. He reveals more of Himself to us. "The more we pray, the more we think to pray, and as we see the results of prayer—the responses of our Father to our requests—our confidence in God's power spills over into other areas of our life."[8]

Seed Habits

Just like devouring the Bible, devoting ourselves to prayer can seem like a major undertaking, which is why creating a Seed Habit or two is the perfect way to start. Don't let your desire to have a robust prayer life overwhelm your ability to start small. Seed Habits of prayer will grow. We are working on creating habits—automatic responses—in our ordinary day that lead us to continual connection with our Heavenly Father. With the work of the Holy Spirit, Seed Habits of prayer scattered throughout your day will certainly take root and produce a wild and vibrant garden of prayer.

In chapter two, I told you how I wanted to pray over my kids each day before they went off to school, but I couldn't get the habit to stick. I had to change the formula for that Seed Habit to make it small and easy, but most importantly, to make it fit into my morning routine. The habit wasn't sticking because I hadn't found the right time and place where I'd always remember to pray over my kids. While that Seed Habit only meant a few seconds of prayer for each child, over time it has grown. Almost anytime I touch my children—whether rubbing their backs, guiding them across the street, holding their hand, a quick hug or snuggle—I am prompted to pray. I did not plan or even hope for this to happen. Rather, some sort of Pavlovian effect has taken place in my brain, and when I place a gentle hand on any of my kids, my mind is automatically reminded to pray. Prayer begets prayer.

Just today, my three-year-old was whining and crying because I said she couldn't have something. She was really committed to her act because she followed me around the house, weeping and wailing for several minutes. After multiple attempts to get her to stop, I finally gently reached out to her, thinking maybe if I showed her some compassion and attention she'd stop. Well, right when my hand connected with her little shoulder, I had the thought to pray over her. So right then, out loud, I prayed that God would help her to stop whining and crying and to instead fill her with peace and joy that can only come from Him. I asked that His presence would calm her and help her feel content and happy. I thanked God for hearing our prayers and asked Him to help us have a good day. Do you know what happened? Her attitude and behavior immediately changed! I almost couldn't believe it. But this is what the Lord has slowly been teaching me as I practice a life of prayer. He delights to meet us in the mundane—in the toddler tantrums and the chaos. It brings Him joy to respond to our needs and show us in tangible ways that He hears our prayers.

To pray is to change. Prayer is the central avenue God uses to transform us."

—RICHARD FOSTER[9]

My point in sharing this is that a simple Seed Habit of praying over my kids before they head off to school has supernaturally grown into a life of continual prayer for them and a constant connection to God throughout my day. This is what the Holy Spirit does when we create room for Him—even the tiniest bit.

But Where Do We Practically Start?

Perhaps the best Seed Habit I can offer you is a daily ritual of asking God to increase your desire and ability to pray.

> When I *pick up my toothbrush*, I will ask God to increase my desire and ability to pray.

I love habit-stacking laundry and prayer. I pray for each of my kids as I fold their laundry. I pray for the things I imagine them doing while wearing their clothes (playing with friends, going to school, relating to one another, and so on). I pray for my husband and his needs. I pray for myself. I just let my mind creatively flow from the items I'm actively folding to the prayers I bring before the Lord.

> When I fold laundry, I will pray for the wearer of said laundry.
> When I (insert a specific mundane task like chopping vegetables, loading/unloading the dishwasher, collecting the trash, or sweeping the floor), I will pray for _____.
> When I pull into the car pick-up line, I'll pray for
> _____.

Maybe it's your kids, your marriage, or your job. Maybe you put an index card in your car with a list of five things you want to pray about while in the pick-up line. You could write a new index card each week and keep them as a record of things you've prayed for all year. When a friend asks you if you'll pray for them, you can write them on your index card that week.

When I Wait in Line, I'll Pray for . . .

Waiting in line is a tricky cue because it's not an exact moment in your day (unlike the school pick-up line). However, if you can train your mind to use waiting as a time for prayer, you will never be the same. We wait all the time—in stores and restaurants, in traffic, at red lights, at appointments. We wait for elevators to open, websites to load, and meetings to begin. We wait on hold for customer service representatives. We wait for public transportation, a friend running late, a child to put on his shoes. What if you found one cue that prompted you to pray when you wait, and you let that Seed Habit grow into a constant conversation with God every time you wait? If this is your desire, pray right now and ask God to remind you the next time you're waiting to pray!

Frank Laubach, a Christian missionary and literacy advocate, coined a term he called "flash prayers." Frank felt these spontaneous, quick prayers were one way to pray without ceasing, maintain moment-by-moment connection to God, practice compassion, and co-labor with Christ. If Frank passed a woman who looked stressed, he'd quickly pray that God would overwhelm her with His peace. While walking into a meeting, he'd simply pray, "God, guide our discussion." Essentially, anything that came to mind became a flash prayer to God.

> *When I hear a siren, I'll pray for the first responders and the people they're going to help.*
>
> *When I see an airplane, I'll pray for expedient salvation for everyone on board. That Christ would make Himself known to them and they would all respond in saving faith.*
>
> *When I hear church bells, I'll pray for my pastor and his family.*

When I hear a train, I'll pray for . . .
When I hear a bird sing, I'll pray for . . .
When I hear the ice maker, I'll pray for . . .

Sometimes when I'm truly in the "pray continually" mindset and am constantly sending out flash prayers all over the place, I feel like Hermione Granger with her wand, but instead of zapping out power with magical spells, I am calling on the active Spirit of God. I'm asking His presence to pour over every thing, every situation, and every person around me. I see a little boy wailing at preschool drop-off, and as I walk by him, I pray that God's presence will be palpable to him, that he will immediately stop crying because he feels a sense of peace and love that stops him in his tracks. I pray for the staff member holding him and trying to comfort him while also struggling to protect them both from his kicking and flailing. I pray that she, too, will feel God's presence, and that when the boy stops crying, she will know without a doubt that it is a Holy Spirit moment. I ask that the very experience of that will blow wind in her sails of faith as she, no doubt, faces her own life challenges.

Did the boy stop crying about ten seconds after I prayed my flash prayer? Yes, and his tears were replaced with my own when I was so surprised and overwhelmed by the power of prayer and God's kindness. I prayed for the staff who stood at the exit, asking God to bless them and their day. I prayed for the security guard who held the door as I walked out of the building. I prayed for the mom running in late, clearly frazzled. I just kept praying for every person I saw. It's one of the most fun things I've ever done in secret. Like a giddy child, I feel like I have been given eyes to see people and a power to invite God's Spirit to touch them and encourage them in individual ways.

The best advice I can give when prioritizing a practice of prayer is to start where you're most excited.

If Jesus woke up early in the morning to get away to pray, certainly we also need to prioritize a time of connection with God to lay our anxieties and needs before Him, and also to listen and be in His presence. I've read several books that encourage readers to begin a practice of prayer by setting aside the first five minutes of your morning. If that resonates with you—go for it! Create a Seed Habit like: *When I hit the alarm off button, I will sit in the chair next to my bed and spend five minutes in prayer.* Then let it grow.

But for many of us, the idea of waking up five minutes earlier, pre-coffee, is not enticing. And while perhaps a more traditional teaching on spiritual habits would say, "Just do it! Be disciplined. Surely you can wake up five minutes earlier to spend time with God!" let me take this moment to remind you that the science of habit formation says we have to *want* to do the habit, and it needs to be small and easy in order to create habits that last a lifetime. So, it's okay if you don't want to wake up five minutes earlier to sit in a chair and pray. What do you want to do? What is enticing or exciting? What is small and easy? I believe if you begin praying in the smallest of ways throughout your day, your desire and ability will grow like wildfire. Flash prayers will become your lifestyle.

I have also read many books that advise sitting in a quiet room to focus on prayer. I love this idea in theory, but I personally find this to be the absolute hardest way to pray. When I do practice prayer in this way, I sit still and visualize God on His throne and literally imagine myself approaching Him in His throne room. Sometimes I imagine Him as a mighty king, other times as a Shepherd. Sometimes I visualize all three of the Trinity represented. Other times, I visualize Jesus as I imagine He was as a first-century, thirty-year-old Jewish rabbi. Sometimes I imagine Him as a Physician or Counselor. I use my mind to focus on a visual of Him to keep me focused and grounded in Who I'm talking to.

However, my best, most focused, most vibrant prayer times of any length are when I go on walks. When I am in a difficult season and am starving to be in God's presence, petitioning for my problem or situation, I find my brain telling my body to put on shoes and walk outside before I even realize what's happening. I need to go on a prayer walk. Maybe you already work out consistently, and you decided your Seed Habit is: *After I finish my workout, I will go on a prayer walk for three minutes.*

Don't worry about what you're "supposed" to pray for (missionaries, world leaders, peace in the Middle East), and pray for what you are actually thinking about. Jesus said we all have to approach the kingdom of heaven like a child,* and children never hesitate to say what's on their mind—like, ever. My kids never cautiously ask me for what they need or want—even if it is the absolute worst possible timing. I could be carrying fifty pounds of groceries like a pack mule, determined to get from the van to the kitchen in one trip, and they will stand directly in my way, oblivious to the Herculean feat I am attempting, and ask for a snack. *Are my hands full? Am I in the middle of something?* Those thoughts don't occur to them. They have a want or need, so they ask. They also ask with the confident expectation that I'm going to answer. While they may ask for candy and know there's a strong possibility I'm going to say no, they're still going to ask because they want it, and there's a minuscule chance I'll say yes! They ask with expectation and hope.

> God always meets us where we are and slowly moves us into deeper things."
>
> —RICHARD FOSTER[10]

* Matthew 18:3

When your mind wanders during prayer . . . pray about those things.

When you notice you're rehearsing or imagining a conversation with someone over and over again . . . Stop the role play and bring the entire thing before God. Pray for that person and the situation; pray for wisdom and maturity on your end.

A final prayer prompt I'll offer is to take a common sin or attitude you struggle with and allow that to draw you into prayer.

When I feel angry . . .

When I feel prideful . . .

When I feel selfish . . .

When I interrupt someone else while talking . . .

When I feel overwhelmed or anxious . . .

When I feel judgmental or critical of another . . .

What is your most frequent sin proclivity, and can you use it as a prompt to ask the Spirit of God to transform you? When you feel angry, maybe you ask God to replace it with His peace or to help you forgive. If you feel prideful, perhaps you ask God to help you think of yourself with sober judgment.* If you feel entitled or selfish, ask God to help you consider the interests of others as more important than your own.** This could be a great area for you to find a Bible verse that combats your sin and use it for meditation or memorization as well.

What is just one thing you wish you prayed about more? For me, it was my kids. So my first Seed Habit began there. Maybe it's your job, your marriage, a health concern, or your extended family.

What are the top few things that you constantly find yourself thinking about? What if you created a Seed Habit to begin praying about those things first?

---

* Romans 12:3

** Philippians 2:3–4

> To be a Christian and to pray are one and the same thing....
> It is a need, a kind of breathing necessary to life."
>
> —KARL BARTH[11]

Remember, God gave us prayer as a gift. It's a way to commune with Him, co-labor with Him, increase our faith in Him, cast our burdens on Him, and more. God gave us prayer to take away the weight of the world. Dallas Willard wrote, "Constant prayer will only 'burden' us as wings burden the bird in flight."[12] How many of us are birds walking around the earth on our tiny webbed feet, never to realize He gave us wings to soar?

Chapter Review

- Prayer is an invitation to be in God's presence.
- Prayer is an exercise of faith.
- Prayer is entrusting God with all the things that worry us about this life, knowing He is in control and we are not.
- Prayer is listening. Prayer is allowing the Holy Spirit to guide you and minister to you.
- Prayer is not about your persistence or determination but your dependence on God.
- God cares about your problems, but He uses those problems to bring you into His presence.
- We can approach the throne of God with confidence and like a child. No pretenses. Just come as you are.

Homework

- Answer the questions below:

  - What is one thing you wish you prayed about more?
  - What are the top few things that you constantly find yourself thinking about?
  - Did any cues or habit-stacking ideas stick out to you from the chapter that you'd like to use for your possible Seed Habits?

- Jot down a few Seed Habits you may want to integrate into your day.
- Write your Seed Habits in Dr. BJ Fogg's formula (you may need to reference your chapter two homework): *After I* _____, *I will* _____.
- Optional: Download your free prayer guide at hannaseymour.com/ESH.

Make It Stick

A few reminders from chapter two:

- Make sure your Seed Habits are small, easy, and fit naturally in your day.
- Don't forget your habit will be stickier if you try the 7x method.
- Also remember the benefit of "celebrating" when you are newly practicing your habit.

- Finally, there is strength in numbers. Get a friend to do this with you. Pick three Seed Habits you both want to work on together and share the journey. Even better, pray together! Praying with others is a great way to grow in our own prayer life.

Seeking Solitude

"But he would withdraw to desolate places and pray."
—Luke 5:16, ESV

"The purpose of silence and solitude is to be able to see and hear."
—Richard J. Foster [1]

THE PAPER SHEET COVERING THE EXAM TABLE KEPT TEARING UNDER my legs as I shifted from side to side, attempting to keep my body covered by the thin sheet and exam gown. Tears dripped down my cheeks. I knew I wasn't the first patient to cry in front of this doctor, perhaps not even the first of the day, but I was surprised how quickly the tears came when I began to share how I was feeling.

I was exhausted, drowning in grief, and feeling utterly alone. No one had died. There was no life-altering illness. My marriage was stable; my kids were fine. But something was still deeply wrong in my head and heart. He listened. He asked questions. We talked about thyroid levels, antidepressants, and other variables and options. This doctor knew me well. I'd been a patient of his for over a decade; he'd delivered all three of my babies. He leaned back in his chair and said, "I have an immediate prescription for you, and then we can go from there." He leaned over his prescription pad, jotted down a few words, and handed it to me: *Minimum 24-hour retreat of unplugged solitude.*

What Is Biblical Solitude?

At the height of Jesus's ministry, as massive crowds would gather to hear him teach and be healed, the gospel writers tell us many times that Jesus made it a habit to get away for solitude and prayer.* When Jesus received disheartening news about His cousin John, He withdrew to a secluded place.[2] After a long day of ministry and feeding dinner to five thousand men plus their wives and children, he first sent away His twelve disciples to get them away from the noise and crowds, and then He Himself went up on a mountain to pray alone.[3] Mark and Luke tell us that after another long day of ministry, Jesus woke up before the sunrise to escape to a place of solitude for prayer.[4]

> Jesus was in incessant demand and easily could have been busy all day, seven days a week, if he'd chosen to be. But he didn't; he chose to make time for solitude—going away from everyone to be alone with the Father. Luke 5:16 says this was his habit."
>
> —KENNETH BOA[5]

---

* Take a peek at Matthew 14:13, Matthew 14:23, Mark 1:35, Luke 4:42 and 5:16, and John 6:15.

From sunup to sundown, He was instructing his apostles, teaching the crowds, healing the sick and demon possessed, traveling from town to town, and ultimately preparing the way to His own crucifixion. Yet, in order for Jesus to be faithful to what God had called Him to do, He needed—I believe He craved—time alone with His Father.

If Jesus, the Son of God, needed and prioritized solitude with His Father, how much more do you think we do?

Biblical solitude is not about loneliness, nor is it about being alone with yourself. Loneliness is defined by absence, but biblical solitude is defined by presence—specifically God's presence. It is about getting away from the noise and the crowds for the purpose of being alone with God.

Many times we don't know exactly what Jesus was doing or praying about while He was alone with God, but we do know that He was ushered into a forty-day solitude retreat* by the Holy Spirit as preparation for His public ministry.[6] He also went up on a mountain for prayer and solitude before picking His disciples.[7] Luke tells us He prayed all night! And Matthew tells us how He went to the garden to pray before His crucifixion, taking His disciples with Him, but still secluding Himself from them to be alone with His Father in prayer.[8]

Jesus craved solitude with God before He made big decisions, for preparation before major events, and also for everyday life.

When we study the life of Christ, it's hard to overemphasize how crucial solitude was for Him and His ministry. John Mark Comer believes that solitude was the most foundational of all the practices of Jesus,[9] and after years of studying the life of Christ, Henri Nouwen

---

* Well, he had solitude until Satan decided to show up and tempt Him. A closer reading of the temptation passages (Matthew 4:1–11, Mark 1:12–13, and Luke 4:1–13) may infer that Satan tempted Him all forty days. Regardless, the Holy Spirit led Jesus into the wilderness (*eremos*) and then led Him around for forty days, certainly with full knowledge of Satan's plans to tempt Him, and all for the purpose of preparing Him for the next three years of His public ministry.

concluded that "without solitude it is virtually impossible to live a spiritual life."[10]

I don't know about you, but in many ways, this picture of solitude feels incongruent with my life. I don't have the ability to spend significant lengths of time in solitude. And please don't tell me to wake up an hour earlier than my kids do. Don't you know that if you wake up earlier, your children also wake up earlier? It's some kind of unspoken law of the universe. Also, sometimes prioritizing solitude feels even more than incongruent. It feels diametrically opposed to my role as a mom. God has given me three children to care for and raise. Prioritizing solitude can sometimes make me feel like I'm shirking that God-given responsibility.

It involves intentionally leaving the state of 'being available' to the demands of the outside world and moving to a state of mind and heart in total surrender to and communion with God. It is not the same as the human desire for privacy or a time of quiet. It involves silence and active listening, with a heart listening to God."

—DIANNE WHITING[11]

What Does Biblical Solitude Look Like as a Modern-Day Woman?

So what does solitude look like for the twenty-first-century woman who is running a household, a small business, the PTA, and a literal marathon? When Jesus sought solitude he got on a boat, climbed a mountain, or headed into a garden. Can this spiritual habit of Christ even translate into today's world?

From a biblical perspective, solitude is simply the choice to carve out some time and space to be alone with God. We minimize distractions to focus on being with God. Many times solitude is a "container" habit in which we practice other spiritual habits.[12] In solitude we read and study our Bible. We mediate and memorize God's word. We pray. We worship. We practice gratitude. We practice the presence of God.

But solitude doesn't just have to be a set time in the morning, and in fact, many times this feels impossible for the mom of tiny children, or the nurse, the baker, or someone working any other profession that requires ungodly morning hours.* And even if we're able to have a set time of solitude in the morning, it simply isn't enough to sustain us throughout the day.

Susanna Wesley (1669–1742), perhaps most well-known as the mother of John Wesley (the founder of the Methodist Movement) and Charles Wesley (a prolific hymn writer), was mother to nineteen children, though only ten survived infancy. As she faced the day-to-day challenges of raising children, running a large household, and battling financial struggles,** she couldn't have dreamed of a solitude retreat like so many of our modern-day spiritual discipline books suggest. However, she knew solitude with God was vital to her spiritual health. So what does a mom of ten children do? She would sit down in a chair and pull her apron over her head. I wish I were kidding. That's how she created space and time to be alone with God. Her children knew

---

* I kid about ungodly hours! They're all His, so they're all godly—even if we don't want to be awake and at work at 4:00 a.m.

** Her husband served as an Anglican clergyman, but the family lived in constant financial strain due to his poor financial management, often incurring large debts and even being imprisoned for debt.

if they saw Mom with her apron on her head—leave her alone! She's communing with God!

Now, to be honest, it's hard for me to fathom my kids respecting an apron over my head. Perhaps my firstborn would consider it, but my younger two would probably see it as an invitation to join me under the apron.

Instead, my "Susanna Wesley" moments look more like a minute in the pantry with the door closed and the light off.* Or five minutes in my room, sitting in my grandfather's mustard-yellow chair, with the door locked. I first began this habit when I was battling a toddler's strong will and realized I needed a time-out as much as—if not more than— he did. What started as "Mommy's time-out" turned into moments of solitude as I learned to see my feelings of being exhausted, over- whelmed, irritated, or angry as cues that I needed a moment of solitude with God.

Let me underscore that: I needed a moment of solitude **with God**. I did not need a moment to myself. I did not need a moment to gather myself or to summon my own strength, peace, or patience. I needed to reconnect with the God of the Universe. I needed to commune with the Perfect Parent and rest in His loving presence so that I could be realigned with His heart and love, and then—and only then—get back out there and parent my child.

Solitude is an invitation to remove yourself from your outward cir- cumstances and abide with God in a way that will fuel you to get back in the game. It's a time-out and a team huddle before heading back onto the field. Donald Whitney calls these "minute retreats."

Solitude gives us the space to quiet the noise and demands around us and to align ourselves with the heart of God, to seek His wisdom

---

* Sometimes it may or may not include a Trader Joe's dark chocolate treat or a beef stick.

and guidance, and to receive His strength, love, and resources to fill our empty tanks so that we can be faithful to whatever God is calling us to do that day.

Solitude Can Be but Doesn't Have to Be _____

Solitude can be for an extended period of time. Many authors on the topic of spiritual disciplines extol the virtues of weekends away in solitude. My doctor agrees! Jesus, Moses, Elijah, David, Paul, and many others went out into desolate places for extended periods of time. But solitude can be for a shorter time frame, as we read was Jesus's frequent habit, and it can even just be for a minute here or there.

In an extremely rare moment, I found myself home alone. I decided to curl up on the couch and spend some time reading a novel. Only a few minutes later, the thought entered my head (keep in mind I was fully engrossed in the story) that I was in a quiet house and I had the opportunity to enter God's presence in silence. *Wow, okay,* I thought. I laid my book down, got off the couch, and knelt over the ottoman. *Okay, Lord, I'm here. I will sit here until you say something or release me.* I spent the first few moments simply imagining being in the Heavenly Holy of Holies. I imagined the Triune God on His throne. I imagined myself on the court floor before Him, face on the ground. I waited and knelt in silence. Sometimes that's all it is. A quick moment of silence and solitude before Him. Some days, and that day in particular, He gave me a simple picture of something I needed to hear from Him. He spoke to a lie I had been believing and gave me a new prayer to bring before Him.

Another time, I was making my bed as I do every morning. While making your bed is a great ordinary habit to pair with a Seed Habit, it's one I have yet to anchor any spiritual habit to. Yet on this particular day, out of nowhere I just sensed an invitation to stop and kneel in silence. I was in the middle of putting the throw pillows on and stopped mid-placement. I almost finished making the bed first and then laughed, thinking, *God doesn't care if the bed is fully made.* I spent maybe sixty seconds in silence, solitude, and stillness before Him. I imagined Him leading me as the Good Shepherd beside still waters on a beautiful sunny day, in the shade of a tree. And that was enough. I asked Him to lead me throughout my day, and I finished making the bed.

Solitude can be still and quiet, but it can also be amidst movement and even noise. A great time for solitude with God is during a walk, run, hike, or other physical activity where your mind can be elsewhere. Years ago, I heard a pastor share about an excruciatingly difficult season in his life when the only time he felt like he could meet with God was while running. He needed the visceral movement, his feet pounding on pavement, sweat pouring from his brow, for Him to be vulnerable enough to enter the presence of God and honestly commune with Him.

Solitude can quite literally be anywhere. Many of us have had experiences on a mountain or a beach, or a place where we were enveloped in God's glorious creation and overwhelmed by His presence. Susanna Wesley sat under her apron. Sometimes I sit in my pantry or car. Some authors write about solitude of the heart and mind. You may not be physically distant from other people or noise, but you are able to tune it all out in such a way that you are alone with God.

Similar to practicing the presence of God, there are actually dozens of moments throughout our ordinary days when we could be experiencing moments of solitude with God. However, we have a powerful, pervasive enemy at work against us. It's so effective that Cal Newport writes, "It is now possible to completely banish solitude from your life."[13] Yet avoiding the spiritual habit of solitude comes at a great cost.

The Enemy of Solitude

The average person checks their phone 205 times a day.[14] Depending on age, Americans spend anywhere from three and a half to six hours a day on their phones.[15] If you are anything like the average person in the Western world, from the moment you wake up to the moment you go to sleep, you are paying attention to your phone. It is likely the first thing you touch when you wake up, and once you silence your alarm, you swipe on over to check the news, the weather, your emails, or social media. You haven't even gotten out of bed but you've invited the entire world to be with you—and many times scream at you—while you're still in your pajamas. The noise is already deafening.

You scroll on your phone while you walk to the bathroom, brush your teeth, and wait for coffee. You check your phone while you're driving. You reach for it while you wait for the meeting to start, while you wait in line at the coffee shop, while you sit in the carpool line. You scroll to "take a quick break" from whatever you're doing at work or at home. You check it almost incessantly when it vibrates or makes a noise. You reach for your phone when your friend runs to the restroom and leaves you alone at the table. You scroll at the dinner table, even while your spouse or kids are talking to you. It's the first thing you reach for when you sit on the couch at the end of the night after the kids are in bed, the kitchen's been cleaned, and you can finally put your feet up for the day. You even scroll while you're watching TV. And of course, you check it one more time before you go to sleep, or you scroll for an extended amount of time trying to fall asleep.

For years, I had been blaming my experience of "brain fog" on being pregnant and raising small children, when I began to wonder if it had more to do with the distraction and noise of my environment, but specifically my phone. How many times have you grabbed your phone to do something—shoot a quick text, add an item to your grocery list, buy something off Amazon—and suddenly found yourself in another app or two for several minutes, or even forgotten what you were doing altogether?

We Are All Overwhelmingly Distracted

"For many of us the great danger is not that we will renounce our faith. It is that we will become so distracted and rushed and preoccupied that we will settle for a mediocre version of it. We will just skim our lives instead of actually living them."

—JOHN ORTBERG[16]

At least twelve times in the New Testament, we are exhorted to stay alert. In Colossians, Paul urges his readers to set their minds on things above, not on earthly things,[17] and if we believe the data (which I do), it would be fair to say we set our minds on our phones. In Philippians, the apostle encourages his readers to think on, dwell on, and set their minds on things that are true, lovely, honorable, excellent, pure, and praiseworthy. While you could argue that there are some of those things to be found on our phones, for the purpose of our conversation on solitude, I would say we are giving our attention to our phones instead of the very presence of God.

In his book *The Ruthless Elimination of Hurry*, Comer writes:

. . . what you give your attention to is the person you become. Put another way: the mind is the portal to the soul, and what you fill your mind with will shape the trajectory of your character. In the end, your life is no more than the sum of what you gave your attention to. That bodes well for those apprentices of Jesus who give the bulk of their attention to him and to all that is good, beautiful, and true in his world. But not for those who give their attention to the 24-7 news cycle of outrage and anxiety and emotion-charged drama or the nonstop feed of celebrity gossip, titillation, and cultural drivel. (As if we "give" it in the first place; much of it is stolen by a clever algorithm out to monetize our precious attention.) But again: we become what we give our attention to, for better or worse.[18]

Ruth Haley Barton, in *Invitation to Solitude and Silence*, writes that desperation is often what draws us to solitude. We've tried everything. We read our Bibles; we spend time in prayer. We attend church as much as we're able. We're doing the things we know to do for the spiritual life, but is that all there is? We're exhausted; we're lonely; we're underwhelmed. Something has to change, but what else is there?

If you can learn to replace your instinct to check your phone with an instinct to check in with God, you will radically change your life.

Instead of grabbing your phone as the very first act of your day, you say your Seed Habit morning prayer of gratitude and submission and instantly paint your day with God's will. As you walk to the bathroom, you have a moment of solitude with God. You read your Bible while your coffee brews. You meditate or work on Bible memory while you brush your teeth. You don't touch your phone while driving. Instead, you don't even turn on music because you use the time for solitude, or you turn on worship music and use the time for gratitude, worship, or prayer.

Instead of reaching for your phone while you wait for the meeting to start, you do "flash prayers"* for everyone in the conference room, or on the Zoom call, and you do it again while you wait in line at the

---

* We discussed flash prayers in chapter four, in case you've forgotten or skipped that chapter. It's an idea coined by Frank Laubach in which we are in constant communication with God, specifically in petition for people we see as we go about our day.

coffee shop. In the carpool line, instead of grabbing your phone, you find the three-by-five cards where you've written verses you want to pray over each of your kids. Whenever you need to take a break and "check out" for a moment during the day, you tune in with the Lord instead of social media. You practice His presence and spend the time you need realigning your heart with His. You are renewed and refreshed because you spent time with Him instead of doomscrolling on your phone, which only depletes you even more. You've turned off almost all the notifications on your phone because you realized they were only distracting you from what was in front of you.

When you're at dinner with a friend and she runs to the restroom, you sit at the table in a moment of head and heart solitude. You're not physically alone or without noise, but you can shut it out for a moment. You don't need to look at your phone to amuse yourself while she's gone. Instead, you have the ear of the Creator of the Universe bending down to listen to you. You never scroll at the dinner table, especially when your spouse or kids are talking to you, because you refuse to have your phone anywhere near you during that sacred time. At the end of the day—once the kids are in bed, the kitchen's been cleaned, and you finally put your feet up—you meditate on your verse again, or simply sit in silence before the Lord, or you check in with yourself or your spouse. *How are you doing? Like, really doing?** And of course, you dock your phone away from your bed, well before lights-out time, because you've learned it's good for you to physically distance yourself from it (no matter how many boundaries you put up, it has a siren song), and you close your eyes at night with a simple prayer: *Okay, it's you and me,*

---

* If you're checking in with yourself, bring whatever you're thinking and feeling before the Lord. *God, I am flat-out exhausted—why? What do I need from you, or is there a change I need to make? Lord, I am depressed—show me what's going on in my head and heart. God, today was the best day ever! Let me just sit in gratitude before You.*

Lord. What do you want to discuss? And you let Him lead your thoughts and prayers until you fall asleep.

We become what we give our attention to. Are you paying attention to your phone, or are you paying attention to the things of God? Who are you becoming?

Seed Habits

If you feel a little angsty or even annoyed with me right now, I get it. I just came after your phone habits. But please hear me say that I was just as guilty, if not more guilty than where you're standing.

I remember the first time I thought, *Something has to change with my smartphone usage,* and it had nothing to do with my spiritual habits and everything to do with parenting habits. I heard a therapist talk about how kids are impacted by their parents' smartphone usage and was horrified. My kids were taking a backseat to my phone. I was missing out on moments, not making eye contact, and sometimes flat-out ignoring them because my phone had my attention. As we discussed in chapter one, our daily habits naturally lead to our outcomes. I was on a path to becoming the kind of parent I didn't want to be. I was on a path of raising kids who had a distorted view of managing technology because their mom didn't model good boundaries with her own.

If I may rephrase a question I asked you in chapter one: **Who do you want to become, and what small spiritual habits can you start to help you get there? And are there any habits you need to uproot and throw out of your life?**

When it comes to creating Seed Habits of solitude, I want you to consider your smartphone habits and how those may be distracting you—not just from opportunities of solitude, but from opportunities for a life tethered to God and His goodness.

Jesus invited his apostles to "come away by yourselves to a desolate place."[19] They were hungry and tired, exhausted from their work, and constantly surrounded by crowds of people and noise, and Jesus invited them to get away to a quiet place for rest and renewal. In Matthew, he invites all who listen: "Come to Me, all who are weary and burdened, and I will give you rest" (Matthew 11:28, NASB).

Jesus is inviting you to come away to a quiet place and spend time with Him in solitude.

> As daily sleep and rest refresh the body, so daily silence and solitude refresh the soul."
>
> —DONALD WHITNEY[20]

Remember our steps to creating a sticky Seed Habit: Make it small, make it easy, make it fit, let it grow. Keep in mind the formula: After I _____, I will _____.

After I make my bed, I will pause for a moment of solitude with God.

After I finish my workout, I will go on a three-minute walk as a time of solitude with God.

After I pour my cup of coffee, I will pause for one minute of solitude with God. (Maybe you need to hide in your pantry or—better yet—can you step outside?)

After I sit down to eat lunch, I will pause for a minute of solitude and connection with God.

After I touch my phone, I will immediately put it down and take one minute to practice solitude with God.

After I read a difficult text or email (and before responding!), I will pause for a minute of solitude.

After putting the kids to bed, I will pause at their door (or out of eyesight if this will cause an issue) for a minute of solitude and reconnection with God.

After I feel overwhelmed, angry, irritable, or (fill in the blank), I will walk away from the situation and give myself two minutes of solitude with God.

If you want to really shake up your relationship with your smartphone, here are a few ideas to begin with:

- Stop sleeping with your phone nearby. Buy an alarm clock and keep your phone as far away from you as you can handle.
- Decide how long you want to be awake before you let yourself touch your phone.*

---

* My personal rule is about two hours. I don't let myself touch my phone until I grab it on the way to our home gym. I use my phone to track my workout, so that's the first moment in the day I truly "need" it. (Though certainly I could track my workout differently.) At times I have different boundaries for when I'm allowed to open social media apps, email, news, etc.

- Consider a Seed Habit where you replace your morning phone scroll with Bible intake. You could create an identity-based goal by saying, *I am a person who reads her Bible before she ever checks her phone.*
- Find a place in your home and at work where your phone lives. You don't need it on your body. You don't need it with you at all times. Keep it in that spot unless you actually need to use it, then put it back.
- Use screen time settings to limit your time on any app that is a distraction to you.

Summary

- Biblical solitude is about getting away from the noise and the crowds for the purpose of being alone with God.
- Biblical solitude often includes silence and stillness, but it can also include movement and even be experienced amidst noise.
- Jesus is inviting you to come away to a quiet place and spend time with Him in solitude for rest and renewal.
- Biblical solitude is often a "container" habit because it leads us to other spiritual habits like prayer, biblical intake, practicing the presence of God, gratitude, thanksgiving, worship, and more.
- Your phone is distracting you and possibly leading you down a path of natural outcomes that you do not want.
- If you can learn to replace your instinct to check your phone with an instinct to check in with God, you will radically change your life.

Homework

- Will you start right now?

  - Spend one minute in silence and solitude. Find a posture that works for you—maybe you sit, kneel, or lie down.
  - Or can you go for a quick walk around the block? Three minutes of solitude with movement. Just keeping your mind in God's presence. Imagine Him walking right alongside you.

- Locate special places where you can have a moment of solitude.

  - Is there a specific chair in your house?
  - Is it your pantry?
  - A back porch?
  - Is there a bench somewhere close by in your neighborhood?
  - The bathroom?

- Answer the prompts in your workbook:

  - How do you distract yourself or prevent yourself from experiencing solitude? When does this most often occur for you?
  - How do you feel about your current smartphone usage? Do you need to make a change? What will be your first small, easy Seed Habit of change?

Make It Stick

A few reminders from chapter two:

- Make sure your Seed Habits are small, easy, and fit naturally in your day.
- Don't forget your habit will be stickier if you try the 7x method.
- Also remember the benefit of "celebrating" when you're newly practicing your habit.
- Finally, there is strength in numbers. Get a friend to do this with you. Pick a Seed Habit you both want to work on together and share the journey.

CHAPTER SIX

Toasting to Joy!

THE PRACTICES OF CELEBRATION AND THANKSGIVING

"To miss out on joy is to miss out on the reason for your existence."

—Lewis Smedes[1]

If you're a mom, you know the signs: They begin to move very slowly, complain something on their body hurts, insist they're starving (like you haven't fed them two meals and two hundred snacks already), and their sweet little voices transform into ear-bleeding, mind-numbing whines. Their gas tank is empty, and you're still a good ten-minute walk away from the parking lot as you try to navigate the crowds at the zoo.

"Do you need a power-up?" I'll ask the wilting child. "Okay, better hold on tight!" I say enthusiastically, as I grip their little hand in mine. I begin to squeeze tighter and tighter, shaking their arm faster and faster, while I make "energy-surging" noises (you'll have to use your imagination) until it climaxes into a sound of explosion. "Do you feel infinity times more energy? Stronger? Faster?" I ask, eyes wide open.

A smile, a nod, sometimes an energetic "YES! Thanks, Mom!"*

As Richard Foster so beautifully states, "Celebration brings joy into life, and joy** makes us strong."[2]

Amidst a weary world, in which we encounter brokenness at every turn and battle exhaustion most days, joy is the secret sauce to our endurance. Joy is what fills our empty tanks. Joy is what gives us a power-up and makes us feel infinity times more energy and strength.

The spiritual habits of celebration and thanksgiving are the keys to unlocking joy in our lives.

We want to have more joy in our day-to-day lives. We want to be more joyful, especially during hard times, but we can't just clap our hands and say, "Okay! I'm going to be joyful!" This goes back to us *trying* to be like Jesus instead of *training* to be like Him. When we practice habits of celebration and thanksgiving, we train our hearts and minds to be joyful. We submit ourselves to God's Spirit, who grows our capacity for joy and ability to be joyful.

What Is Biblical Celebration?

When King David successfully brought back the Ark of the Covenant to Jerusalem (after it had been taken by the Philistines over twenty years earlier), he celebrated in a way that you and I might think is not very becoming of a monarch. Certainly, Queen Elizabeth wouldn't have

---

* I'm just imagining doing this with a teenager and cackling out loud. I realize this is a toddler to young elementary–age trick, and its shelf life is short, but by golly if I won't use it until it has been rendered utterly ineffective.

** This comes directly from the Bible: "The joy of the Lord is my strength!" (Nehemiah 8:10).

participated. He danced and leaped before the Lord with all his might; he and the other Israelites shouted like their favorite football team had just clinched the Super Bowl win in the last few seconds of the game. Trumpets blared. Then the king offered burnt offerings and peace offerings to God and passed out three different kinds of cake to the entire kingdom to take home and have a celebration with their own families. Talk about a party!

The Hebrew word used in this story that we translate into "celebrate"[3] is *sechoq*, which means "laughter in merriment or defiance." David was certainly laughing and celebrating in merriment, but could it also be said that he was laughing in defiance of the previous twenty years, when the symbol of God's presence was missing from Jerusalem? Just prior to this, David had attempted to get the Ark back home, but he hadn't studied up on how God required the Ark to be handled. Unfortunately, this cost a man's life. Was he now celebrating the goodness of God that delivered the Ark back home in defiance of the terrible struggle and hardship to get to this moment?

> Celebration heartily done makes our deprivations and sorrows seem small, and we find in it great strength to do the will of our God because His goodness becomes so real to us."
>
> —DALLAS WILLARD[4]

It might feel rebellious to say we are celebrating in defiance, but doesn't joy amidst suffering seem a bit rebellious? It's not a rebellion against God; it's a rebellion against our broken circumstances and an evil world.

Shauna Niequist wrote, "Celebration is a tap dance on the fresh graves of apathy and cynicism, the creeping belief that this is all there is, and that God is no match for the wreckage of the world we live in."[5]

In his commentary on the book of Philippians, which is a letter about joy in the most dire of circumstances, Karl Barth describes joy as a "defiant 'nevertheless!'" No matter how bad things seem, we can list our sorrows one by one and conclude it all with: *Nevertheless, I have joy because of my hope in Jesus!*

Biblical celebration is the expression of joy no matter our circumstances. It is the declaration of joy rooted in the goodness and faithfulness of God.

> It is the discipline of choosing gratitude rather than grumbling and remembrance rather than indifference. . . . Celebration, whether individual or corporate, is taking pleasure, amazement, and joy in how good God has been to us in specific ways and times.
>
> —KEN BOA[6]

When we celebrate, we open our eyes to a new perspective.

The Bible opens with celebration and closes with celebration, and it's woven all throughout the text. After each day of the creation account in Genesis, God saw His creation was good (He celebrates) and then declared the seventh day as a day to rest from work and marvel at the work of His hands (another celebration). Then, in Revelation we see a vivid portrayal of a magnificent feast where God will fully dwell with His people and creation. He's handing out way more than three cakes per family! There will be no more tears, no more pain, only joy, love, and great celebration.

Throughout the Old Testament, God commanded His people to remember and celebrate. Three annual festivals*—called "feasts to the Lord"—required the nation of Israel to travel to Jerusalem to offer sacrifices, corporately remember what God had done for them, and thank Him for His provisions. The Feasts of Weeks and Tabernacles were specifically feasts of joy and thanksgiving. In addition to those three annual feasts, God's people were commanded to observe and celebrate continually throughout the year through the Sabbath (every week) and New Moon celebrations (every month), which included the blowing of trumpets and banquets.

When Jesus came onto the scene, he was ushered in with celebrations as a multitude of angels proclaimed the great news and praised God before a few terrified shepherds. His first recorded miracle was at a celebration—a wedding—and His last night before facing the cross was a celebration of the Passover with His closest friends.

God designed remembrance, gratitude, and celebration to be part of His people's consistent rhythms. While this is ultimately for our good, it's also because our God is a God of joy.

Too often we think of God as angry or sorrowful, or at the very least, just an incredibly serious God. While the Bible may tell of moments when God is angry or filled with sorrow, it is always in response to a fallen world. Yet God in His very nature is joy. In fact, as noted by Richard Foster, "Jesus rejoiced so fully in life that he was accused of being a wine-bibber and a glutton."[7] While we don't need to run after negative reputations, as followers of Jesus, we should be the most free, alive, and joyful people on the planet.

---

* The Feast of Unleavened Bread (Passover), the Feast of Weeks, and the Feast of Tabernacles

John Ortberg wrote, "The joy we see in the happiest child is but a fraction of the joy that resides in the heart of God."[8] Do you believe that? If we are image bearers of God, the unbridled joy a four-year-old can express is only a glimmer of the joy her Creator possesses. If this is true—and I believe it is—how vastly do we underestimate God's capacity for joy? When God has the final say, when evil has been irrevocably destroyed and He makes all things new, all that will be left is joy—for both God and us.

So we train our capacity for joy (and become more like Him—our Joyful God) by celebrating throughout our days on earth.

> We engage in celebration when we enjoy ourselves, our life, our world *in conjunction with* our faith and confidence in God's greatness, beauty, and goodness."
>
> —DALLAS WILLARD[9]

Celebration can also be an act of defiance amidst our broken world when we boldly declare God is good, and we trust Him to care for us and provide for our needs.

As I approached the completion of my seminary program, a friend asked, "So when's the party?" My first thought was, "I'm not throwing a party." Completing my master's was just a stepping stone to a greater educational goal, and it honestly hadn't crossed my mind to celebrate it in any significant way. However, the more I thought about it, the more I realized it still was a significant milestone that was worth celebration.

Not just for me, but for my family and friends who had been part of the process and supported me along the way.

The first celebration happened right after I wrapped up my final oral assessment. I walked out of my home office to find my husband and three kids hiding in the kitchen, armed with homemade confetti and giant smiles. They showered me with rainbow-colored paper and began a kitchen dance party to a Jonas Brothers song.* Then we headed out for ice cream at the "*expensive* place."** While I didn't need to go out for ice cream, my husband insisted our kids needed to participate in a moment of celebration to mark this milestone in our lives. Celebrating God's goodness and faithfulness in our lives is just as much about others as it is about us. I don't know if they'll remember the two and half years when their mom was often studying in her home office early in the morning or late at night, but they, too, were part of the journey and made sacrifices for me to pursue that degree. They needed to celebrate their own part in it, and they also needed to see their parents practice the habit of celebration.

The second celebration was one of the best nights of my life. We threw a dip-loma party, where everyone was required to bring their favorite dip. My husband made a signature cocktail (punnily called a Summa Cucumber Laude), and we had a mini–graduation ceremony in which my dad (a former president of a Bible college) officiated, pomp and circumstance played, and regalia was worn. It truly was a night of joy and celebration, but the best moment was when my husband opened the floor for toasts. Before anyone could toast me, I jumped in to explain that while the night was certainly a moment of celebration for me, I hoped everyone would go around the room and share one

---

* The song is titled "Celebrate!" and it's a vibe!
** Jeni's! This was no moment for Sonic.

thing they were also celebrating. It could be something as small as "my child slept past 6:00 a.m. today"* or as large as "I finished my master's degree!" But after each person shared, we would all raise our glasses and say, "To the goodness and glory of God!"** I am tearing up just thinking about it. Friends shared celebrations of a benign tumor, experiencing peace that surpasses understanding, a new job, a five-year-old daughter who scored two soccer goals that morning, and even the Dodgers' World Series win—all to the goodness and glory of God! It lasted over a half hour, as person after person went around and raised a glass to joy. We celebrated in merriment; we celebrated in defiance; and I think, right there in that moment, our capacity for joy increased. We practiced in shared celebration and our joy grew.

What Is Biblical Thanksgiving?

While many authors will divide celebration and thanksgiving—or will only discuss one, essentially combining both practices under one name— I believe they are two distinct practices that are intricately related. If joy were a coin, one side would be celebration and the other thanksgiving.

> Be joyful always; pray continually; give thanks in all circumstances, for this is God's will for you in Christ Jesus (1 Thessalonians 5:16–18, NIV).

Most of us spend an awful lot of time worried about what God's specific will is for our lives, and while I understand the good desire behind that, scripture spells out His will of desire for us very clearly in several passages, including the one above. God's will for your life is to

---

* This is a true celebration in my home.
** My brother-in-law joked about getting tattoos that night: TTGAGOG. I'm still open to it.

be joyful always—not just when the sun is shining, birds are chirping, your children are all perfectly behaved, everyone you love is healthy, and overall things are going your way. It's His will that you are *always* joyful—no matter what. It's His will that you pray continuously, and it's His will that you give thanks in all circumstances. Once again, Paul nails us with an *all*. *Always* and *all*—he doesn't mince words.

This verse tells us that the way to experience and exude joy *always* is through the practices of prayer and thanksgiving. When we make prayer and thanksgiving a habit—an automatic behavior—joy is the result.

In a different letter to a different church, Paul wrote, "Don't worry about anything; instead, pray about everything. Tell God what you need, and thank him for all he has done. Then you will experience God's peace, which exceeds anything we can understand. His peace will guard your hearts and minds as you live in Christ Jesus."[10]

I've heard this passage preached (more than once) as a command to stop worrying. *"Be anxious for nothing! Don't worry!"* Yet, how many of us have nipped anxiety in the bud by simply yelling at ourselves, *STOP BEING ANXIOUS!** It just doesn't work like that, and of course God knows that.

When Paul wrote this to the church in Philippi, he was prescribing the way to fight anxiety and experience peace. We replace our anxiety by cultivating habits of prayer and thanksgiving. Little by little, seed by seed, drip by drip, we create a lifelong habit of remaining in the presence of God with gratitude that will expel fear and anxiety.

The practice of gratitude or thanksgiving has become a hot topic in the scientific community over the last decade. Multiple studies show a strong correlation between gratitude and life satisfaction.[11] The

---

* I wasn't feeling anxious at all, but now after writing those three words in all caps, my body is physically reacting. I have a knot in my stomach and my chest feels tight.

practice of gratitude has been linked to improved mental and physical health, quality of relationships, and a general feeling of purpose and a meaningful life.[12] It also is linked to lessening negative conditions like depression, anxiety, phobia, bulimia, addictions, negative emotions, dysfunctions, anger, and hostility.[13] In fact, studies show gratitude begets gratitude.[14] So biblically and scientifically the results are in: When we practice gratitude, our lives improve.

The twenty-five-year-old version of me is mortified that forty-year-old me drives a minivan. At twenty-five, I wasn't sure I wanted children, but on the off chance I did have them, I would have bet my entire life savings that I would never, ever, ever, ever drive a minivan. To make matters worse, I love my minivan. Twenty-five-year-old Hanna would hang her head in shame.*

But you know what happened when I pulled out of the dealership with my brand-new black Honda Odyssey? I started noticing black Honda Odysseys everywhere. Every street I drove on, every parking lot I turned into, there they were. *Where two or three Honda Odysseys are gathered in my name . . .*** It was like all of a sudden, the world was teeming with black Honda Odysseys.

This is called the Baader-Meinhof phenomenon, or more commonly the frequency illusion. There are two parts to this cognitive bias. The first is that because of your new awareness of something (a new vocabulary word, a car, a concept you learned, a brand), that thing suddenly appears to increase in frequency all around you. The second part is a confirmation bias where you believe that the frequency has actually changed. The truth is that there were always a ton of Honda Odysseys out on the road. I just didn't notice them until I had a reason to notice them.

---

* I know some of y'all completely relate, and those of you who don't (because you still refuse to drive a minivan), you just don't know what you are missing!

** Just checking to see if you're still with me.

The same is true when we practice gratitude. The more we practice gratitude—the more we intentionally look for God's goodness and faithfulness in our lives—the more we'll see it. Not because the frequency changes, but because we have become more aware.

There is a joke in my family that "God loves Kailey." Kailey is my darling sister-in-law. Years ago, as she planned her wedding, everything kept going her way. Things that shouldn't have worked out did; things that should have cost more cost less. Literally every tiny piece worked out in her favor. Everyone who witnessed this would simply shrug and say, "God loves Kailey." The week leading up to her wedding, heavy rain was forecast. Naturally, just moments before her wedding, the clouds parted, the sun came out, and not a drop of rain fell. *God loves Kailey.* After Kailey and her equally darling new husband whisked off in their getaway car, my husband began to break down the wedding rentals and load up a trailer. As he did, the skies opened and a deluge of water fell down upon him. "God loves Kailey, but why doesn't God love me?" he jokingly cried out.

This is the Baader-Meinhof phenomenon at its finest. Kailey, and everyone around her, just so deeply believed God loved her that everything went her way. When the rain came, my husband immediately (but jokingly) jumped to the conclusion that God didn't love him. Of course this is a silly story, but it is also true of how most Christians live.

Either we move about our day noticing and thanking God for all the ways He blesses us—for His goodness, faithfulness, and trustworthiness—or we don't. Either we see confirmation after confirmation of His love for us, or we don't. If we are in the latter group, we aren't simply not noticing, but we are also reiterating a confirmation bias that God cares about other people, but not us. Thoughts pervade our mind like: *Everything goes wrong in my life. God never answers my prayers. God always seems distant from me. I know He loves me, but*

He doesn't seem to like me. If this is what we keep telling ourselves, it's exactly what we'll continue to see.

On the other hand, gratitude begets gratitude because we see more and more things to be thankful for. The absence of gratitude begets cynicism, discontentment, and eventually anger and bitterness.

In a psychology journal, authors described gratitude as "a life orientation towards noticing and appreciating the positive in life."[15] As followers of Jesus, we have been called to orient our lives around Jesus, noticing and thanking God for not just every good gift, but for everything.

Whatever is good and perfect is a gift coming down to us from God our Father . . ." (James 1:17).

"Give thanks to the Lord, for He is good; His faithful love endures forever" (Psalm 136:1).

"And whatever you do or say, do it as a representative of the Lord Jesus, giving thanks through him to God the Father" (Colossians 3:17).

". . . when troubles of any kind come your way, consider it an opportunity for great joy" (James 1:2).

"We can rejoice, too, when we run into problems and trials, for we know that they help us develop endurance" (Romans 5:3).

Biblical thanksgiving is expressing gratitude to God for His goodness and faithfulness in all circumstances.

I once had a pastor who said her dad would thank God every time he stubbed his toe—"THANK YOU, JESUS!" While we may scratch our heads and think that's ridiculous, it's a whole lot better than some of the words that have come out of my mouth when I've slammed my toe into the corner of my bed or stepped on a forgotten Lego. Is thanking God in that moment of pain gratitude in defiance of the pain? Could we be declaring, "Even in my pain, God is still good!" or "Thank God I have a toe to stub!" Certainly some of you are rolling your eyes* or think I am over-spiritualizing this—and maybe I am—but how is that different from James urging us to rejoice amidst troubles, problems, and trials? We aren't thanking God for the hardship. We don't thank God for sin or a broken world (or toe), but we can thank Him because even when surrounded by challenges, He is good and faithful, and He uses those circumstances to transform us into Christlikeness.

Before we jump into how we can create Seed Habits of celebration and gratitude, I want to submit one final idea to you about the nature of our thanksgiving. Certainly, we can and should thank God for the stuff of life—coffee, a warm house, a cozy bed, our children, a good job, a body that can move, provisions for our physical needs. But I want to caution us from thanking God for these things in comparison to those who don't. Many times you'll hear people say something like "Well, thank God I have a house" (unlike a homeless person), or "Thank God I have children" (unlike my sweet friend who has struggled for years with infertility), or "Thank God I live in America and not the Gaza Strip."

During the first century, right when Jesus came to earth as a baby, it was customary for Jewish men to begin each day in prayer: *Thank you, God, that I am not a Gentile, a woman, or a slave.*

---

* I'll admit I'm chuckling a bit.

We read that and think, *Oh my gosh, how awful! How politically incorrect! How bigoted!* Yet, in a way, that's exactly what we're doing when we thank God in comparison to those who we think don't have it as good as we do. However, the homeless person can still thank God. The woman struggling with fertility can still be grateful. The families struggling to survive in a war-torn country can still praise God for His faithfulness. The paraplegic can still rejoice in God's goodness. When we thank God for our earthly blessings in comparison to what we deem as someone else's earthly loss, we diminish their ability to rejoice in God, and more importantly we minimize God's goodness to our personal definition of blessing.

So, we can still thank God for the things we have—because it all came from Him—but we have to be careful that our gratitude isn't based on having more than others.

Seed Habits

In the realm of psychological research, practices that increase gratitude are known as gratitude interventions. Common gratitude interventions consist of gratitude journals, gratitude lists (also known as TGT—Three Good Things), and writing notes of gratitude to people in your life.

As a reminder, when we create Seed Habits we must choose habits that we *want* to do. While this may seem obvious, it's wild how often we don't do this. We want to clean up our diet, so we choose to implement a habit where we eat an afternoon snack of celery instead of popcorn. I don't know about you, but nothing about that sounds appetizing to me. While that may be headed toward the outcome I want, if I don't really like celery, that is going to be a painful (and eventually failed) Seed Habit.

The same goes for practicing gratitude. If keeping a journal of any length on a regular basis feels like pulling teeth (*Hi! Hello! It's me!*), then do not make that your Seed Habit.

Here are some ideas to get you started:

- Journal for one minute every morning when you first wake up (remember to use the formula: After I _____, I will write in my gratitude journal for one minute).
- Journal for one minute before you go to sleep each night. (After I get in bed, I will . . .)
- Write down one to three things you are grateful for each morning or night. (Studies show that people who do this before bedtime have less stress and sleep better!)
- After a person randomly comes to my mind, I will send them a quick text that says I'm grateful for them, citing one reason.
- After I put the keys into the ignition, I will thank God for three things.
- During transitions throughout my day (after I leave my house, the gym, or work, or after a meeting and after picking up my child from school), I will take one minute and reflect on things I can thank God for from that part of my day.
- After I sit down at the dinner table, I will think of one thing to thank God for or to celebrate from the day. If I'm with friends or family, I will ask everyone to share. (TTGAGOG)
- When I do something I loathe (fold laundry, load the dishwasher, etc.), I will replace my grumbling with

gratitude by thanking God for everything that comes to mind for at least one minute.

- After I am annoyed by something (my husband didn't wipe down the counter, my kid blatantly ignored or disobeyed me for the fifth time today, my coworker forgot—again—to loop me in on an important conversation), I will take a deep breath and think of one thing to be grateful for specifically about the person who annoyed me.

Years ago, a friend taught me to always keep a bottle of champagne in my refrigerator so that I would be ready to celebrate at any given moment. She hosted a weekly Bible study where we frequently had something to celebrate—an answer to someone's prayer, a new job, a successful first date, an academic achievement or passing of a licensure exam, a promotion, a difficult conversation gone well. The rhythm of collectively sharing our celebrations (always with a glass of bubbly) created a culture of joy often in both merriment and defiance. While we raised a glass, hard things were still happening—others in the group were experiencing loss or painful circumstances—but by sharing our joys we reminded one another to hold fast to our good God.

Maybe your first step toward celebration is simply: Tomorrow when I leave work, I will buy a bottle of bubbly so I am ready to toast to the goodness and glory of God!

While we can certainly intertwine celebration with gratitude to create Seed Habits of celebration that fit into our everyday routine, practicing celebration can also happen on a less frequent but larger scale.

- You could host a quarterly potluck (or keep it even simpler, drinks and dessert—or dips!) with your closest friends that is all about sharing celebrations (big and small).

- My sister-in-law came up with the idea of "proud of you parties." Host a party for a friend (could be as simple as getting a date on the calendar and a dinner reservation with a small group of friends) because you are proud of her. Maybe she's persevering through a hard time. Maybe she just got a new job. Maybe she did something really brave. Or maybe it's not a party for one person, but you get your closest friends together, and everyone shares one thing for each person that they are proud of. We can encourage one another by celebrating one another and God's work in our respective lives.

- When it comes to celebrating holidays, think about how you could be more intentional about celebrating God's goodness in those moments. The way most of us celebrate Easter always makes it seem like a pretty lame holiday to me (when you compare it to Christmas or even the Fourth of July or Thanksgiving). How could you make Easter a more intentional celebration of the death and resurrection of Jesus?

- Maybe you make Friday nights a celebration night. No matter where you are or who you're with, you ask everyone to celebrate something from the week. If you have small kids, have a "Celebrate!" dance party and have everyone shout out things they are grateful for and want to celebrate.

Chapter Review

- Celebration and gratitude are the keys to joy and are two sides of the same coin.
- Biblical celebration is the expression of joy no matter our circumstances.
- Biblical thanksgiving is expressing gratitude to God for His goodness and faithfulness in all circumstances.
- Our God is a God of joy, and if we want to be more like Him, we need to train our capacity for joy through celebration and gratitude.
- Celebration and gratitude beget celebration and gratitude, and they ultimately grow our capacity for joy.
- God in His infinite goodness and joy implemented times of remembrance, celebration, and gratitude for His people.
- We should be the most joyful people on the planet.

Homework

- Ask yourself, *Am I a person of joy? If not, what needs to change?*
- Define one or two Seed Habits that will cultivate a habit of gratitude or celebration in your ordinary day. Write them down below along with when you plan to implement them.
- Extra credit: Pick a date on the calendar right now to host a quarterly celebration or "proud of you" party and text some friends to save the date. TTGAGOG!

Make It Stick

A few reminders from chapter two:

- Make sure your Seed Habits are small, easy, and fit naturally in your day.
- Don't forget your habit will be stickier if you try the 7x method.
- Also remember the benefit of "celebrating" when you're newly practicing your habit.
- Finally, there is strength in numbers. Get a friend to do this with you. Pick a Seed Habit you both want to work on together and share the journey.

CHAPTER SEVEN

Cultivating Friendship

"It is not good for the man to be alone."

—GENESIS 2:18

"Friendship is, for many of us, one of the most important but least thought about aspects of life."

—DREW HUNTER[1]

AS SOMEONE WHO HAS DEVOTED HER ENTIRE ADULT LIFE TO PURSUING deep friendships, I nervously, and a bit ashamedly, confessed to my mom that I felt lonely. While I had a number of women I could name whom I dearly loved and called close friends, I was in a new season of life— a mom of two toddlers and a baby, working part-time outside of the home, and unable to find time to even call a friend. I had transitioned from a job where I worked closely with a team of people I considered dear friends to a very independent role. I went from being around adults most of the time to having my days largely consumed by three tiny terrorists. When I was around adults, I either acted like a conversation-ally starved person—talking too fast, sharing too much, and coming across a little unhinged—or I had zero conversational abilities whatsoever. My brain was gray matter, my memory gone. While some moms got together for "playdates," I found it too challenging with my work schedule combined with the baby's and toddlers' nap schedule, and if I'm being really honest—I kind of hated playdates anyway. I always left them feeling exhausted from wrangling my kids while simultaneously trying and failing to have adult conversation. I was at a loss. I knew how to make friends and cultivate friendships. I mean, I had friends. Yet, I felt so lonely.

"You're in the lonely years," my mom said gently.

The lonely years are when your head is barely above water while you're raising young kids. People don't invite you over for dinner anymore because hosting a family feels like a lot, and it's hard to meet friends out for dinner because you need a babysitter. Your evenings revolve around dinner, bath, and bedtime, so your social life is limited. Weekends are spent doing who knows what (I can't even remember), and suddenly it's Monday again and you're on to a new week of surviving without any real connection to friends.

You may be in the exact same lonely era, or your life may look entirely different from what I just described, yet you still would title it "the lonely years."

We Are So Lonely

In late 2024, 20 percent of US adults reported feeling loneliness "a lot of the day yesterday."[2] Another poll in 2024 found 30 percent of adults said they have experienced feelings of loneliness at least once a week over the past year.[3] In 2023, the surgeon general declared a loneliness epidemic in the US, and in 2025 stated that loneliness "can cause deep pain—and is a major health issue."

Loneliness can increase:

> . . . our risk of heart disease, dementia, premature death, but also our risk of anxiety, depression, and suicides. Loneliness is a source of deep pain in people's lives. We are made to connect with one another, to be a part of something bigger than ourselves. And when we lose that, we do feel, like, a deep sense of pain.[4]

Loneliness is literally killing us. Another study[5] found that more than four out of five people (82 percent) reported that their friends (and the people they spend the most time with) don't know them deeply. The same percentage also said they don't feel very close to those friends. Nearly one-third said their friends don't know them at all or have surface-level relationships. And, terrifyingly, more than half (54 percent) reported they don't have a friend they feel comfortable calling in the middle of the night with an emergency.

In his book *Building a Non-Anxious Life*, Dr. John Delony likens this to not having insurance or a financial emergency fund. He says:

> Half of you have no one to call, even in case of an emergency. Imagine your body laying down to sleep every night and the deep-seated part of your brain responsible for keeping you alive looks around and recognizes you have nobody to help you out if you're overcome with a full-blown asthma attack. Or if you were to slip coming out of the bathroom at 4:00 a.m. It's like waking up to find yourself with no place to call home. Or no

insurance. Or no emergency fund. This is you without a safety net, and your body knows it.[6]

You and I need a 2:00 a.m., just-a-phone-call-away friend, and we also need friends who fully know and love us, and we them.

The Habit of Friendship

Written in all caps, in blue ink, on the front page of my dad's Bible is:

> *Remember:*
> *Everybody needs a friend.*
> *Everybody is under-encouraged.*

You may think that's an odd thing for a pastor and Bible teacher to write in the front of his Bible. Or maybe you'd think he was more of a self-help, faith-light guru rather than a no-nonsense, verse-by-verse expositor. But believe me when I tell you he's the latter. He's committed to a historical-grammatical study of the text, will teach you several Greek or Hebrew words in the course of one sermon, and by the end, you'll feel like you sat through a mini–theology class when it's all over. Yet after a lifetime of walking alongside and shepherding people, he continues to see the need in every single person without fail: Everybody needs a friend. Everybody is under-encouraged.

For three years, I had the privilege of serving in Slovenia for a couple weeks each summer. A team of youth and adults from my local church would travel to Eastern Europe to support a youth ministry that hosted summer camps for Slovene teens. When traveling, there are always dozens, if not hundreds, of fascinating cultural differences you notice. But one thing that immediately stood out to me when chatting with Slovene teens was how rarely they called people "friend."

"Ana is my classmate. Luca is my neighbor. This is Maja; I know her from choir. Aleksander works with my brother."

I asked one of my new Slovene *friends* why they rarely used the word. "Oh! You Americans," she laughed, "you call everyone your friend. A Slovene only calls one to three people their friend over the course of their entire life." She went on to explain that they reserved the word "friend" for only a few people with whom they have a deep, meaningful, time-tested friendship.

There's something about that I really like. Most of us use the word "friend" for almost every single person we know. And while that may seem friendly or just easier than identifying people in other ways, I wonder if it hasn't depleted the true meaning of friendship for us. If a friend can be almost anyone, then it means almost nothing.

In his book *Made for Friendship*, Drew Hunter says:

> Most of what we call friendship is little more than acquaintanceship. But acquaintanceship is to friendship what snorkeling is to deep-sea diving. Snorkeling is fine, but skimming along the surface isn't exploring the deep.[7]

Do you have at least one "deep-sea diving" friend? Someone who really knows you? They know your past, your present, and your hopes for the future? They know your strengths and weaknesses, your giftings and your sin struggles? When you're having a hard day, you can shoot them a text and ask for prayer or a literal helping hand. You can cry in front of them. They show up for you; they support you; they cheer you on. They see you doing the hard things. When you spend time with them, it fills up your cup. Just being around them puts wind in your sails. You can go deep with them; you talk about spiritual things. They point you to Jesus. They encourage and motivate you to press on and stay faithful to what God has called you to do.

If you do, amazing! I'd encourage you to write their name(s) down right next to that paragraph. We'll come back to those names at the end of the chapter.

If not, please don't despair. For the remainder of this chapter, I want to consider what it might look like to cultivate a habit of friendship. I want to challenge us to value and pursue friendships differently. I want to show you how God created us for friendship and uses friends to lighten our load, deepen our joy, and grow us in our own spiritual maturity.

Created for Connection

Before the beginning of time, before mankind or the universe existed, there was God and there was community. The Triune God—Father, Son, and Spirit—has eternally existed as three persons in one unified God. Within the Trinity, God has given us a picture of perfect community, that which is central to His own character and goodness.

In the first chapter of Genesis, God says to Himself, "Let us make man in our image, after our likeness."[8] Theologians have spent a lifetime trying to define what it actually means to be made in the image of God, and there is much discussion about it, but I believe one way we were created to be like God is to be a reflection of His community.

But the emphasis of community in Genesis doesn't stop there—as the narrative continues, we learn that God made Adam first, only to proclaim that it isn't good for the man to be alone. I imagine when this part of the story was being told to the nation of Israel it was a record-scratching, somebody-hold-the-phone, could-have-heard-a-pin-drop moment. Over and over in Genesis chapter one, God created, He saw what He created, and He declared, "it was good." But then, after He makes man and puts him in the garden, God says out loud to Himself, "It is not good for a man to be alone." Creator of the Universe, say what?! This is not how the story was patterned to go. This is not what the audience was expecting to hear. No, God wanted to emphasize that solitude is not His plan for mankind. The man needed a helper,* and thus begins community, unity, relationship, and friendship between people.

We were created for connection. God never intended for us to do this life of faith independently. We are not meant to follow Jesus on our own. In fact, we cannot mature in our faith alone. It's not the way God designed it. God created us for community, and He uses the soil of community to produce growth in our lives. Without it, not only will we not grow, but we will wither and die.

A Traditional Approach

In many books on spiritual disciplines, you will find a chapter on "community" or "fellowship." This has been the traditional label of "doing the Christian life with others." While it makes sense that we need one another, it might surprise some of us that community is frequently listed among the traditional spiritual disciplines. You might think, *Community should just be organic! You become friends with some other believers and voilà! Community!*

---

* Don't get mad at this word! The same Hebrew word used in the Genesis text to describe woman as "helper" is the same Hebrew word used to describe the Holy Spirit in reference to us! The Holy Spirit is our helper, and there is no way you can flip that to mean the Holy Spirit is subservient or less than us. He is fully God! We need His help in the same way a man alone needs help. To be a helper isn't weakness, but strength!

But when we really consider the current state of our own Christian community, most of us will readily admit it's not as easy as it seems. It takes work, effort, commitment, and practice. In fact, community never just happens. It is always built.

This is why so much of the New Testament discusses how to do Christian community—how to serve one another, care for one another, and ultimately love one another as God loves us.

A traditional teaching on the practice of community would emphasize the importance of participation and service with your local church. It would likely include small groups, accountability partners, discipleship, mentorship, and more. It would emphasize the two main analogies the Bible gives us about the Christian community—the body of Christ and the family of God. It would also discuss how in community we also practice several other spiritual habits, such as Bible study, prayer, celebration, worship, confession, service, and many others.

I think this traditional teaching is absolutely vital and relevant for today. I want you to be involved in a local church body. I want you to participate regularly and serve joyfully. I want you to be known by people at your church. I want you to experience the joys and tensions of small groups and learning to love people simply because they are your brother and sister in Christ, and not because they are people you are particularly drawn to be friends with. I want you to learn to practice spiritual habits with other believers because it helps us grow in those areas. I want this for you because this is part of how God designed us to live out our faith in today's world.

As Adele Ahlberg Calhoun writes, "God's family is meant to be the 'show and tell' of what true belonging and love looks like."

We need each other, and the world needs us to need each other.

But I believe a smaller piece to the larger practice of community is the habit of friendship. When we scatter Seed Habits of friendship into our days, we cultivate a life of being known and loved, of knowing and loving others—and those habits will grow into lifelong connection with the family of God.

On the flip side, you can be involved at your local church, you can be faithfully serving your brothers and sisters in Christ, and you can still not have a life of meaningful friendships.

And God knows we need friends. He programmed it into our DNA.

Biblical Friendship

J. C. Ryle wrote, "This world is full of sorrow because it is full of sin. It is a dark place. It is a lonely place. It is a disappointing place. The brightest sunbeam in it is a friend. Friendship halves our troubles and doubles our joys."[9]

When we have real, sunbeam friends (not casual, surface relationships, but plumb-the-depths, full-heart friends), they lighten our load and increase our joy. The Bible shouts of this all throughout scripture:

Rejoice with those who rejoice; mourn with those who mourn (Romans 12:15, NIV).

Carry each other's burdens, and in this way you will fulfill the law of Christ (Galatians 6:2, NIV).

. . . encourage the disheartened, help the weak, be patient with everyone (1 Thessalonians 5:14, NIV).

. . . so that we can comfort those in any trouble with the comfort we ourselves receive from God (2 Corinthians 1:4, NIV).

The heartfelt counsel of a friend is as sweet as perfume and incense (Proverbs 27:9).

In my late twenties, I went through a difficult breakup. My heart was completely broken and, though it feels dramatic now,* I remember feeling like I had lost all hope for that area of my life. While I sobbed in the arms of my dear friend, she just sat with me for a while and eventually said, "It's okay if you don't have any hope. I have enough hope for both of us. You can borrow some of mine." While the pain of that moment has long since disappeared, I have never forgotten her words. A true friend is one who sits with you in grief but holds enough hope for you to share.

In that same week, another dear but long-distance friend called me up with a last-minute trip to the Bahamas. She and another friend had booked it, and they were looking for a third to split the hotel. *Actually, that would be amazing*, I thought, and then shared with her the news of my recent breakup. Years later I found out the whole thing was a ruse. There had never been a Bahamas trip in the works. My friend had simply heard through the grapevine that I was heartbroken and thought a last-minute trip to the Bahamas might give me a little joy. So, she found a last-minute deal, pulled in another friend, and there we were bathing in the sun just a few weeks after my breakup. A true friend goes out of her way to show up for you (even when you don't directly tell her you need help!) when you really need it.

In Christian circles, we often talk about how God created marriage as a picture of Christ and the church, but God also created friendship as a picture of His relationship with us. Drew Hunter unapologetically states:

> . . . friendship is the ultimate end of our existence and our
> highest source of happiness. Friendship—with one another

---

* Thank God for perspective and a testimony that He had something much better in store for me.

and with God—is the supreme pleasure of life, both now and forever, and no one can fully enjoy life without it.[10]

Ultimate end of our existence? Highest source of happiness? That feels pretty dramatic, but think about it. God created us for friendship. Jesus, who was often referred to as a "friend to sinners," explained to His disciples that He came to befriend them.* He declared,

> This is my commandment: Love each other in the same way I have loved you.
>
> There is no greater love than to lay down one's life for one's friends.
>
> You are my friends if you do what I command (John 15:12–14).

While the Pharisees may have called Jesus a "friend to sinners" as an insult, Jesus came as a friend to sinners because He came to lay His life down for every man, woman, and child. He is the perfect picture of love and friendship, and He calls us His friends when we love and obey Him. But the theology of friendship doesn't stop there. Jesus commands His friends to love one another in the same way He has loved us. To lay down our own lives for one another—not to literally die—but to consider others as more important than ourselves,[11] to know each other fully, and to love one another despite our unlovely parts. That is precisely what Christ did for us.

In 2023, dozens of blogs and podcasts became all abuzz discussing if "therapy-speak" was ruining our friendships. Story after story was shared about how friends broke up with friends or set up very rigid

---

* "I no longer call you servants. . . . Instead, I have called you friends" (John 15:15, NIV).

boundaries in the name of "self-care." Boundaries are important,* and nowhere in scripture are we told to be a doormat for others, but if you find yourself in a friendship where you are only considering your needs—not only is that not biblical, but you're just being a bad friend. Or perhaps we should say you're not being a *friend* at all.

And this is where things get interesting, because we all want deep-sea-diving friendships. We all want a friend we can call at 2:00 a.m. if our house is on fire. We all want a friend who fully knows us and fully loves us. We all want a friend who shows up and supports us. But are we all willing to be that kind of friend?

It takes work, time, and sacrifice. It requires that you think of someone else's needs and consider them as more important than your own!** I don't know how shocking that idea was to first-century Christians when Paul wrote it in his letter to the Philippians, but boy does it scream countercultural for us today.

You're telling me I have to consider someone else's needs as more important than my own?! What about self-care?! Boundaries?! Prioritizing my Maslow's hierarchy of needs?!

The Apostle Paul is saying, *Stop being selfish and instead have a humility that allows you to consider other people as more important than yourself.* He's not saying they are more important, but rather showing us the opposite of a self-centered life. We can be self-centered or others-centered. There's no other option.

Yet he goes on to say, "Do not merely look out for your own personal interests, but also for the interests of others."[12] He's not saying, *Deny every interest and need you ever have and put others' needs and wants above your own.* He's just saying, *Don't be selfish! Think of other people and consider how you can show up for them.*

---

* Thank you, Dr. Henry Cloud!
** Philippians 2:3–4

The reason we can live a life that is others-centered, without anxiety or fear that no one will be looking out for us, is that we have a Heavenly Father who is always considering not just our basic needs, but what is absolutely best for us. He knows what you need before you know you need it. He is your provider and sustainer. So, you don't need to worry about putting yourself first, because He will take care of you.

Also, true friendship goes both ways. When you have a friend going through a hard season, you show up for her. You bring her dinner. You take her kids to the park to give her a break. You help her declutter her house or go through the attic. You just sit with her. You spend time with her. And someday, whether it's months or years later, she'll have the privilege of doing the same for you.

In 2023, I went through a dark season. In the beginning I suffered silently; I didn't want to drag down my husband or my friends. But after the stormy clouds continued to persist week after week, I realized I needed to let others in. So I sent out a text message—an SOS—to a handful of friends.

Hi! This is just me letting you know that I'm having a hard time. [I listed out several things I was facing.] It's just a lot of changes, a lot of moving parts. I feel like I'm having to juggle more things than ever before with less support than ever before. To put it bluntly, I feel alone in life. I am not okay.

The text went on for a while, but you get the gist. Over the next year, the friends I texted—they carried me and our friendship. They checked in on me, encouraged me, were patient with me, and physically showed up in a variety of ways to lighten my load. I had nothing left to give, but they loved me all the same.

That's real friendship.

Where to Begin

While we may feel like our capacity for friends can ebb and flow over the years, our need for friends stays the same. Friends aren't a luxury, they're a necessity. So no matter what stage of life we're in, we can begin creating small, easy habits that fit into our day and that will mature our snorkeling friendships into deep-sea-diving relationships.

My dad's note in the front of his Bible* didn't stop as just another observation he made or an insight he was given. Instead, he has relentlessly pursued a life of meaningful friendships. These men span over decades of his life. Some he's known since childhood, others he's met only in the last season of life, but all of them he has consistently and tirelessly pursued and cultivated deep friendships with. While I believe my dad is an extraordinary guy, and the quantity and quality of his friends are rare, I believe we can all have friendships like he has if we're just willing to put in the effort.

Because the secret to having great friends begins with you. You have to be a good friend. Ghandi said: *Be the change you wish to see in the world.* I say: Be the friend you wish you had.

Perhaps that feels a bit reductionist, but you have to be convinced that one, a life of great friendships is possible for you, and two, you are not only capable of cultivating those friendships, but it is completely up to you. When I consider the dozen or so women in my life who have faithfully stayed beside me for years, I'd say only a few of them initially pursued me. That means the other ten or more women, whom I dearly love, would likely not be part of my life had I not first pursued them. And thank God I did! Because they are all women who have held up my arms when I was too tired, who have spoken truth—sometimes encouraging, sometimes convicting—over my life when I needed it

---

* Reminder: Everybody needs a friend. Everybody is under-encouraged.

most. God has used them to grow me immeasurably, and hopefully I them. They are closer than a sister. But all deep friendships begin with one person who identifies, pursues, and encourages. Will it eventually become reciprocal if it's a worthwhile friend? Yes, but someone has to go first.

Identify

Whether you have a hundred surface friends, a dozen best friends, or zero friends, I want you to begin by taking inventory of the friends and friendships you currently have and what kind of friend you have been. Take a moment and write down a list of your closest friends.* If that feels discouraging, write down a list of anyone you consider a friend or who you'd like to be better friends with. On a scale of one to ten, how close are you with these people? Do they really know you? Do you really know them? Go back to the beginning of this chapter and reread the paragraph that describes a true friend.

Consider where you know these people from. Is it work? School? Your kids' school or activities? Your neighborhood, gym, or church?

Circle a few people** you want to pursue a deeper friendship with. Maybe there is a hole you see—you want to cultivate a friendship with someone on your street. Go ahead and write their name down. They may barely be an acquaintance now, but you've identified them as some-one you want to pursue.

When I first moved to Nashville, that is how I continually eval-uated the brand-new friendships I was cultivating. Who had I met in

---

* Remember, I have a free workbook for this!

** Start with two or three, but no more than five. For some of you, it will be hard to limit the number. You simply cannot pursue a lot of close friends all at one time. I know you want to, but you simply cannot. You are limited. Different seasons allow you to pursue different friends, so over the years I believe we can cultivate lots of close friends, but it takes the span of time to do so. So, for now, just choose a few. Start with three.

the last month? Did any of those women stick out as people I wanted to pursue a deeper friendship with? I met a ton of people; I said yes to lots of invitations; I initiated spending time with other people. I got to know my coworkers. I got involved at a local church. I just observed and waited until I started identifying women I really wanted to know better.

Pursue

Then, you have to pursue people. Pursuing people means going after them until you catch them. While not every person you pursue will result in a meaningful friendship, it's the only way to know if they will or not. Pursuit looks like asking a new friend to join you in an activity you enjoy (hopefully they like it too!). Maybe you ask them to go on a walk or hike, to take the kids to the park,* grab a coffee, or even ask a few friends (even if they don't know one another!) to all go out to dinner for a girls' night.

A few years ago, I got the wild idea to invite three other moms in my neighborhood to do a six-week group where we met with a life coach. The life coach had a different topic of conversation each week to help us explore things like our priorities and values, where we might need help, and things we wanted to change. While the life coaching itself wasn't something I desperately needed, I did desperately want to get to know some women in my neighborhood better. This seemed like a quick way to do a deep dive with a few women, but with a fairly low time commitment. All four of us loved our six sessions together, and while we didn't continue to meet weekly, we had dinners monthly for a while, and they are still women in my neighborhood I reach out to and continue to pursue.

---

* Unless you're like me and hate playdates.

Pursue Relationally

Pursuing goes beyond initiating time with a person, it's about pursuing someone below the surface level. It's about asking questions that go beyond what's filling your calendar, upcoming trips, the weather, and what you're binging on Netflix. It's about moving beyond sharing information to sharing our hearts.

Now, I know I just lost some of you, because sharing our hearts sounds absolutely vulnerable and potentially awful. But to be in a real friendship with someone—a friendship that matters, a friendship that God will use to lighten your load, double your joy, and grow you in your walk with Him—you have to let them all the way in. You have to let them actually know who you are in order for them to fully love you. If you never unveil your heart, if you never let someone all the way in, they can't fully love you. And deep down you know that. God fully knows you and fully loves you, and He designed genuine friendship to be a reflection of that.

While my memory is terrifyingly fading the older I get, I have a visceral memory of sitting in my therapist's office in my mid-twenties confessing I was afraid that if I ever let someone truly in, to know me fully and completely, they wouldn't like me anymore, much less love me. While I had some great friends, and I was a good friend to many people, I kept everyone at arm's length. They thought they knew me, but I had carefully curated and controlled what they knew about me and what I kept hidden in my soul. I never knew what it felt like to just be fully and completely myself and to let someone choose to love me anyway. In an attempt to protect myself and avoid vulnerability, I had closed myself off to true love, friendship, and freedom.

The Apostle John tells us, ". . . if we walk in the Light as He Himself is in the Light, we have fellowship with one another, and the blood of Jesus His Son cleanses us from all sin" (1 John 1:7, NASB). Written in the margin of my Bible next to that verse is: "Exposure = Freedom." Not only does stepping into the light give us access to Jesus's payment for our sins, but it gives us the ability to have real community, real friendship with one another. Stepping into the light means being real, transparent, and vulnerable.

While there may be many elements that compose the soil of friendship, including time, common interests, shared values, and others, I would argue that vulnerability is the main fertilizer. Without vulnerability, there cannot be true friendship. Have you ever tried to connect with someone and when you ask how they're doing they only give cursory, surface-level answers? After asking a few different ways, not only do you give up trying to decipher how they're really doing, but you also don't feel like you can share what's going on in your life either. When we pretend everything is fine, we cut off the other person's ability to be truthful about their life circumstances. And here's the deal—everyone has hardship. Your hard is different from my hard, but we've all got it. True friends ask about and share what's hard.

While writing this chapter, I had a conversation with a friend who said she thinks the recovery community does friendship better than any other community—including the church. *Of course they do!* I thought. The recovery community is built upon vulnerability. You can't be in a recovery community unless you can admit you need help and everything is not fine. A lot of the Christian community, on the other hand, tries very hard to look like they've got it all together and *everything is absolutely fine, thank you, Jesus!** True friendship can only exist when we

---

* Of course, not every church or Christian community is this way—thank God! But I do think there is truth to the stereotype of everyone pretending they have it together when they walk into the church building on Sunday morning.

are completely honest with another person about how we are doing—work, marriage, kids, finances, spiritually, emotionally, mentally—we leave nothing in the darkness.

And you, dear reader, if you want that kind of friendship, you are going to have to lead people into the deep waters. Most people have never had a real, vulnerable friendship where they are fully known and fully loved. Maybe you haven't either—and that's okay! You don't have to be an expert in vulnerability to simply be honest with what's going on in your life and ask your friends questions that allow them to share as well.

Years ago, I decided I was going to stop asking friends "How are you?" I was tired of getting surface answers. When I spend time with a friend, I want to go deep, quick. Frank Laubach* wrote in his diary:

> I disapprove of the usual practice of talking "small talk" whenever we meet, and holding a veil over our souls. If we are so impoverished that we have nothing to reveal but small talk, then we need to struggle for more richness of soul.

HALLELUJAH, FRANK! I have never liked large group gatherings or parties because there is just so much small talk, and it physically exhausts me. Give me a one-on-one, and I am there! Give me a dinner party for six and I'm there! But once the group gets too big, meaningful conversation becomes nearly impossible. I don't want to waste time with small talk! That doesn't mean it has to be all serious; in fact, we laugh a ton! But I don't want to share information when I'm with my friends. I want to share hearts.

---

* Our "flash prayers" guy from chapter four.

Pursue Christ-Centered Friendships

While reading and organizing my thoughts for this chapter, I took a quick inventory of my own friendships. A few names came to mind of women I wanted to invest in more deeply. But I also realized that one of my closest friends—someone who has shown up for me through thick and thin—is someone I've never intentionally pursued a Christ-centered friendship with. This is where the habit of friendship truly becomes a spiritual discipline.

You can have deeply genuine and loyal friends, but if they aren't friendships that point back to Jesus, we are missing the best part. God created us for friendship. He created friendship for us to enjoy, and for us to enjoy God through friendship. The friend who "sticks closer than a brother"* is the friend who encourages you, champions you, challenges you, and pushes you in your spiritual growth. Spending time with them somehow makes us feel like we've been in the presence of God—not because they are God! Far from it! But because we see a reflection of who God is through them.

Pursuing Christ-centered friendships means you make it your mission to spiritually edify and encourage one another in your walks with Jesus. You remind one another of God's truth. You spur one another on toward love and good deeds (Hebrews 10:24). You pray for one another, celebrate wins, carry burdens, and continually point one another back to Christ.

As I was taking my own friendship inventory, I made a decision that I was going to be intentional about pursuing a Christ-centered friendship with a woman who already means so much to me. Now, that may seem intense or scary, but all I did (my very small, easy step) was to text her: *How can I be praying for you?*

---

* Or sister! (Proverbs 18:24).

Ask Good Questions

It's honestly that simple. Ask your friends how you can pray for them, and follow up about the things they share. Ask them what God is teaching them in those situations or in their current life circumstances. Ask them how they prioritize their relationship with Jesus, or what their Bible reading or prayer life looks like—not out of judgment, but curiosity. In the same way I have asked several friends: How do you get laundry done? Do you have a system? What does meal prep and grocery shopping look like for you? Is there anything you do on a regular basis to intentionally spend time with your kids instead of just keeping them alive and handling the logistics of getting them through the day? These are questions I ask friends because I'm looking for ideas. I'm rethinking how I'm doing these things and wondering if there is a better way. Why don't we ask similar questions of our friends regarding our spiritual habits?

Be the friend who asks good questions. How's your anxiety level? Are you content with your season of life right now? What do you find yourself thinking about all the time? What are you worried about? How's your marriage? What's the most difficult relationship you have in your life right now? What do you think God is asking of you right now?

Encourage

The third and final step of building meaningful friendships is encouragement, and to be honest, if you're pursuing a friend well, then they are already going to be encouraged—and you will be too! But to intentionally encourage means to be their cheerleader, show up for them when they need you, be a listening ear and a shoulder to cry on, be a sounding board. Ultimately, be the kind of friend you want! If you have a friend who puts the wind in your sails, think about what it is they do and how you can be that same kind of friend.

Sometimes I wake up in the middle of the night with a random person on my mind. I decided years ago that this must be an invitation from the Holy Spirit to pray for that person. Not too long ago, I was woken up several times to pray for an old friend of mine. This was someone who was a very dear friend at one point in life, but due to job changes and life changes, we are rarely in touch anymore. Nothing bad happened—just life! After a few nights of being woken to pray for him, I sent him a quick text:

> I just wanted you to know that God sees you and is working on your behalf. I believe that one of the ways the Holy Spirit helps us and advocates for us is by enlisting other people to pray for us, and I am here to tell you—He has tapped my shoulder for you. Hope that encourages you, my brother!

I probably don't need to tell you that my text was exactly what he needed to hear at the precise moment he received it. It never ceases to amaze me how God works like that. That text cost me nothing. Even praying for him cost me nothing except I suppose a little sleep, but instead it gave me everything. My hopes were buoyed, my tether to God was strengthened, and the combination of prayer and a simple text meant everything to that friend.

Friendship is not rocket science, but it takes time and effort. It means allowing someone else's needs to inconvenience you. It means considering other people's needs as more important than your own. It means wading into the waters of vulnerability and sharing your heart and your hardships with another. But the life-giving joy you will receive from having those friendships will be your buoy when the storms of life overwhelm. They will lighten your load and double your joy, and

God will use them in mighty ways to grow you and shape you into His likeness.

Seed Habits

Establishing and deepening friendships is not a small, easy thing. It's not something we can accomplish in two minutes or less. And while we can make it fit into our day, sometimes we need to interrupt our day for a friend. But if we want to be a good friend and we want to have meaningful friendships, we can still create Seed Habits that lead us down that path.

Here are a few Seed Habit ideas you could scatter throughout your day that will encourage your pursuit of deeper friendships:

- After I hear a friend's name in conversation or they cross my mind, I'll send a quick "Just thinking of you" text or prayer.
- On Sunday nights, I will text a few friends [name them] and ask them how I can be praying for them throughout the upcoming week. (You will be amazed how encouraged a friend will be just by that simple question.)
- But don't stop there! Make a Seed Habit that will help you actually pray for them throughout the week! *After I put on my shoes, I will pray for one of my friends.*
- Every time I drive home from the office or head to the school pick-up line, I'll call a friend just to check in.
- On [insert day of the week], during my lunch break, I'll schedule a meal with a friend who fills my cup or one I want to pursue deeper friendship with.

- On Monday mornings, I'll text a friend, a couple, or another family to invite over for Friday night dinner—it can be BYO takeout! (Choose couples who are life-giving but also ones you can pour into.)
- After I look at my weekly calendar, I'll assign one friend to each day and plan a quick prayer, text, or note of encouragement.
- On the first Monday of the month, I'll send three "Let's get a lunch/coffee on the calendar" texts.
- At 8:00 p.m. each night, I'll respond to any unread texts and send one "just checking in" message to a friend.
- Once a month, I'll invite a few friends for a walk, porch night, or simple gathering (even "bring your own takeout and fold laundry" nights count!).

Recently, I told a friend that I always think of her when I throw away the crust from my kids' peanut butter and jelly sandwiches. As I said it, it struck me—I could turn that habit of thinking about her into a habit of praying for her. A simple Seed Habit could be: *After a friend comes to mind, I will pause and pray for her.*

While this chapter may have painted me as the most thoughtful friend, I can assure you I am very forgetful. I used to say I am an "out of sight, out of mind person"—which isn't untrue, but I decided one day that I didn't want to be that kind of person anymore. So, another Seed Habit of mine is when a friend tells me something that I need to remember, I do at least one of two things.

- One, I say a quick prayer and ask God to help me remember.

- Two, if it's applicable or feasible in the moment, I add it to the calendar on my phone or tell Siri to remind me within a certain time frame.

If you want to create a Seed Habit that encourages vulnerability in your friendships:

- When you're having a bad day, text a friend. Ask her for prayer. (Vulnerability begets vulnerability!)
- After you ask, "How are you?" ask a question that really allows your friend to open up. Reciprocate in sharing.
- After I read my Bible in the morning, I'll text one take-away to a friend who also wants to grow spiritually.

Is there a friend in your life who needs encouragement? How can you show up for her this week? A Seed Habit to be a friend who encourages others could look like this:

- After I walk out of the church building on Sunday (or the gym on Monday morning, or the office on Fridays), I will think about one friend who needs encouragement this week and make a plan on how I will do that.
- After I write in my planner or calendar on Sunday, I'll jot down one friend to encourage that week.
- After I hear my friend is going through a hard time, I will—that same day—write them a note of encouragement and pop it in the mail, or send them a small but fun gift. (I love to send undereye patches, earrings, tea, or a bath bomb.) My dear friend and mentor calls that a

"little happy." As in: *Here's a little happy for my dear friend.*

I mentioned my neighborhood mom group earlier in the chapter.

- Maybe you want to start a very short-term (think low commitment!) group with a few friends. Maybe it's just dinner one time but grows into once a month.
- Is there a book you want to read or are currently reading? Ask a few friends if they want to read it with you and try a one-time book club and see how it goes.

This kind of Seed Habit goes back to our discussion in chapter one about creating identity-based habits. *Who do you want to be?* I want to be a friend who remembers things that are important to her friends and who follows up about them. This is a weakness of mine, so I am slowly (small and easy) cultivating Seed Habits that help me become that person.

What kind of friend do you want to be and what Seed Habit could you implement that would put you on that path?

Chapter Review

- The habit of friendship is the seed to the more traditional practice of fellowship or Christian community.
- Friendship with God and others is the ultimate end of our existence and our highest source of happiness.
- You were created for friendship; friendship was created for your enjoyment, and we enjoy God through friendship.

- To cultivate meaningful friendship we must: identify, pursue, and encourage.
- If we don't connect with our friends on a spiritual level, we miss out on the best part!

Homework

- Identify your existing friends and take an inventory. Are you content with the depths of friendships? Why or why not?
- Identify a few people you want to pursue a more meaningful friendship with.
- Where do you need to start with these friends? Is it pursuing an acquaintance? Is it taking surface friendships to the next level by asking meaningful questions and getting vulnerable? Is it taking a strong friendship to a spiritual level?
- Spend a moment to consider this question: What kind of friend do you want to be, and what Seed Habit could you implement that would put you on that path?

Make It Stick

A few reminders from chapter two:

- Make sure your Seed Habits are small, easy, and fit naturally in your day.
- Don't forget your habit will be stickier if you try the 7x method.

- Also remember the benefit of "celebrating" when you're newly practicing your habit.
- Finally, there is strength in numbers. Get a friend to do this with you. Pick a Seed Habit you both want to work on together and share the journey.

CHAPTER EIGHT

Abiding in Him

PRACTICING THE
PRESENCE OF GOD

"God of all pots and pans and things, make me a saint by picking up the dishes and cleaning up the plates."

—BROTHER LAWRENCE

"Clothe yourself with the presence of the Lord Jesus Christ."

—ROMANS 13:14

IN MY EIGHT YEARS OF MOTHERHOOD, THERE IS NOTHING THAT HAS felt so equal parts easy-peasy and absolutely exhausting as potty training has for me. I have potty trained three children, and all three times I think, *How hard could this be?* And then I'm painfully reminded how incredibly hard it is. But also *it wasn't that bad.* And yet *I'm so thankful I never have to do that again.*

I was potty training my second child, and on day two of the nakey-from-the-waist-down journey, I found myself on my hands and knees, wiping up a puddle of pee from the hardwood floor, and I broke. Tears splashed down onto the floor as I continued to clean. *I'm so tired, God. Do you even see me?* While I did not hear an audible voice, I distinctly felt God's Spirit gently respond: *I am with you right now in this very moment. You are faithfully doing the work I have assigned to you today. This, too, is holy work.*

I sat there, rag in hand, and wept. Not just from exhaustion, but also relief. *He's with me; He sees me; I am doing the work He's called me to do.* Years later, my nose tingles and my eyes water just thinking about it.

God's hand is not so short that it cannot save, nor is His ear so heavy that He cannot hear. Whether you see Him or not, He is at work in your life this very moment. God specializes in turning the mundane into the meaningful. God not only moves in unusual ways, He also moves on uneventful days. He is just as involved in the mundane events as He is in the miraculous. One of my longtime friends . . . often says with a smile, 'God moves among the casseroles.'"

—CHUCK SWINDOLL[1]

Whether you're cleaning your floors (of pee, Goldfish crumbs, or something worse), folding laundry, putting in late nights to prepare for a crucial work presentation, waiting in the carpool line, reconciling bank transactions for your monthly budget, sitting through an hour-long Zoom meeting that could have been a quick email exchange, working out, or mowing your lawn—God is with you. He sees you, and the work you do is holy work if it is done unto Him.

An Awareness of God

In the 1600s, a French soldier named Nicolas Herman was staring at a barren tree thinking about the natural transformation that would take place for the tree from winter to spring. "At that moment he saw clearly the Providence and Power of God"[2] and an all-consuming love of God was placed in his heart. A naked tree revealed the great I AM. Nicolas, who is better known as Brother Lawrence, would reflect back on that day in his teenage years as his moment of conversion—when he suddenly and undeniably recognized the presence of God. Due to an injury that left him partially crippled, Herman was forced to retire from the army, and after a few years, he found his way to a monastery in Paris where he worked in the kitchen for most of his life and was given the name Brother Lawrence. From the trenches of war to the trenches of a kitchen, Brother Lawrence was determined to do absolutely everything—every mundane task of cooking and cleaning—as unto the Lord. He trained his mind to be in constant awareness of the presence of God.

> I would apply my mind carefully to the presence of God, even when I was in the midst of my work. I considered God to be always with me and often in me.[3]

This is what it means to practice the presence of God—to develop a continual awareness of God's presence and to see every moment as an opportunity to be with Him and glorify Him. This moment-by-moment practice created in Brother Lawrence a joy, delight, ease, and radiance that drew others to him. Many people from inside and outside the monastery, from laypeople to nuns to his own superiors, sought his advice and spiritual guidance. Which is why more than four centuries later, an uneducated, lowly kitchen staffer is still teaching men and women of the Christian faith how to practice the presence of God.

> As often as I could, I placed myself as a worshiper before him, fixing my mind upon his holy presence, recalling it when I found it wandering from him. This proved to be an exercise frequently painful, yet I persisted through all difficulties.[4]

Over and over, day in and day out, Brother Lawrence awakened his soul to the presence of God. "We just need to recognize God as intimately present with us and address ourselves to Him every moment."[5] He knew it didn't matter his station in life, whether he was a cook or a vicar, educated or not, during times of mandated prayer and Bible reading or while flipping a cake on the griddle. God is always with us, always loving us; we just need to train our minds to remember and open our eyes to see.

Toward the end of his life, Brother Lawrence wrote, "I make it my practice only to persevere in His holy presence. I do this simply by paying attention to and directing my affection to God. I call this the actual presence of God. It is a habitual, silent, and secret communion of the soul with God. This often causes such joys and raptures inwardly, and sometimes also outwardly, that I am forced to make an effort to moderate them to prevent their appearance to others."[6]

I cannot help but think of how the skin on Moses's face shone so bright after he spent time in God's presence that it frightened the Israelites.* I don't know if Brother Lawrence's face literally radiated, or he was just so filled with joy that it made him giddy, but the king and psalmist David also wrote, "in Your presence, there is fullness of joy" (Psalm 16:11).

In chapter six, we discussed how our God is a God of joy. The core of who He is—His very nature—is joy. So, when we spend time in His presence, truly basking in His goodness and love, the outcome is total joy.

What If Your Entire Life Could Be Continuously Bathed in the Presence of God, in Total Joy?

Dwelling or Abiding in God

While practicing the presence of God may be one of the least talked about spiritual disciplines, I think it might be one of the most helpful and practical habits we can weave into our days. In some ways, the entirety of this book culminates in this one habit. As we devour the Bible, devote ourselves to prayer, find solitude, give thanks and celebrate, and pursue life-giving, Christ-centered friendships, we aim to continually be aware of and in His presence.

If the goal of all spiritual habits is union with God, then practicing the presence of God is the very heart of that pursuit.

In Psalm 27, David writes:

---

* Read it for yourself in Exodus 34:29–35. It's wild!

One thing I have asked from the Lord, that I shall seek:
That I may dwell in the house of the Lord all the days of my life,
To behold the beauty of the Lord
And to meditate in His temple.

David says his sole request of God—the one thing he is after—is that he can *yâshab*, which in Hebrew means to sit down, settle, abide, remain, or dwell in God's presence. While "house" and "temple" could mean the literal tent David constructed for the Ark of the Covenant (which was where God's presence rested), it seems to me that the most logical reading of this is that David is asking for continual, uninterrupted fellowship with God. He longs to go about his earthly life always in the light of God's goodness and beauty.

In John 15, as Jesus is preparing His disciples for His death, resurrection, and impending departure, He tells them that the key to a fruitful, spiritual life is to abide in Him. He uses the Greek word *měnō* ten times in just six verses, which means to stay, abide, dwell, be present, or remain. Sound familiar?

Before Jesus ever stepped foot on this earth, about a thousand years prior, David already knew what Jesus was trying to teach His followers—dwelling or abiding in God's presence is the key to this entire life.

Jesus lands his teaching on abiding with these words: *These things I have spoken to you so that My joy may be in you, and that your joy may be made full.*[7]

To travel back to the words of David: "In Your presence there is fullness of joy."

C. S. Lewis wrote, "We may ignore, but we can nowhere evade the presence of God. The world is crowded with Him. He walks everywhere incognito."[8] The truth is that you and I are already always bathed in the presence of God. It's just whether our eyes are open to Him.

In chapter four, I told you about Frank Laubach and his flash prayers. It will come as no surprise to you that he was also a huge advocate of practicing the presence of God. Early on in his practice, he did an experiment where he tried to think of God while he worked—every half hour, then every fifteen minutes, eventually for one second every minute! This sounds absolutely impossible, but he made it a lifelong practice.

> I have started out trying to live all my waking moments in conscious listening to the inner voice, asking without ceasing, "What, Father, do you desire said? What, Father, do you desire done this minute?" It is clear that this is exactly what Jesus was doing all day every day.[9]

The gospel of John repeats this idea over and over in Jesus's own words:

> Very truly I tell you, the Son can do nothing by himself; he can do only what he sees his Father doing, because whatever the Father does the Son also does (John 5:19, NIV).
>
> Jesus answered, "My teaching is not my own. It comes from the one who sent me" (John 7:16, NIV).
>
> For I did not speak on my own, but the Father who sent me commanded me to say all that I have spoken. I know that his command leads to eternal life. So whatever I say is just what the Father has told me to say (John 12:49–50, NIV).

I could go on. Jesus made it abundantly clear throughout His ministry that He never took a step or said a word that didn't come from His union with God.

As he continued in his quest to remain continually conscious of God, Frank Laubach began to wonder if everyone could practice this constant connection. In a letter to his father, he wrote:

> Can a laboring man successfully attain this continuous surrender to God? Can a man working at a machine pray for people all day long, talk with God all day long, and at the same time do his task efficiently? Can a merchant do business, can an accountant keep books, ceaselessly surrendered to God? Can a mother wash dishes, care for the babies, continuously talking to God? . . . Can little children be taught to talk and listen to God inwardly all day long, and what is the effect upon them? Briefly, is this a thing which the entire human race might conceivably aspire to achieve?[10]

I believe that is exactly what Jesus had in mind when he told his disciples to abide.

Now, don't begin to panic. I am not about to tell you to create a Seed Habit of thinking about God every thirty minutes, much less every minute of your day. But can you see how if you implement a few Seed Habits from other chapters we've covered so far, you will naturally be drawn into His presence more and more? You will automatically begin to think about God more often throughout your day. The Spirit of God, who raised Jesus from the grave and is dwelling inside you, will open your eyes to see more and experience more of Him.

Far too often we wonder and worry about what God's will is for ourselves or for a certain situation. I am here to tell you that it is God's will for you to abide in Him continually. This means if you ask God to do this work in you, He will do it. We see in 1 John 5:14–15: "And this is the confidence that we have toward him, that if we ask anything according to his will he hears us. And if we know that he hears us in whatever we ask, we know that we have the requests that we have asked of him." Jesus told his disciples the very same thing after He explained the vitalness of abiding.[11] When we ask Him for something that aligns with His will, we can have full confidence that He will respond in kind—which means (do I need to spell this out more?) if you ask Him to make you more aware of His presence, constantly remembering Him, thinking on Him, and staying connected to Him, He will absolutely, 100 percent, without a doubt, do it.

> In the noise and clatter of my kitchen, while several persons are at the same time calling for different things, I possess God in as great tranquility as if I were upon my knees in the Chapel.[12]

There have been a few times in my life as a mom—I repeat *a few*—when I have experienced this very thing Brother Lawrence described. I am in my kitchen, no doubt trying to cook or clean, while three different but equally loud children are calling for a variety of things, including, but not limited to: more water, a snack, help on the potty, a report that "he hit me," or just the usual chorus of dramatic whining and nonsense noise. (That's not the part I've only experienced a few times. That's every day, multiple times each day! It's the next part . . .) And on occasion during those times, I have felt the peace of God in such a tangible way that I know He is with me and I smile through it all, graciously and patiently responding to each child without losing my cool. All the while, I'm vividly aware that it is all Him working through me. Left to my own devices, I could never respond like that.

Of course there are many times when I simply respond out of my own flesh—whether that's anger, frustration, or feeling sorry for myself. And there are other times when perhaps it is not as tranquil as Brother Lawrence experienced, but when chaos overwhelms, I simply break out in song and dance: *Holy Spirit, activate, activate, activate! Holy Spirit, activate, activate, activate!* I clap my hands and sort of flail my body around. Usually—even though I've lost count of how many times I've done this—my kids suddenly stop whatever they're doing and just watch in bewilderment. Sometimes they join in, and we continue the song for a minute. Yet no matter what has been happening, or even how my kids respond, this silly little song and dance recenters me. I remember that God is with me; His Spirit dwells within me, and I abide. I figuratively *sit down, settle, remain, be present, and stay* with Him. When I reconnect and abide in His love, I can then respond to the chaos (usually my children) in a way that centers me and glorifies Him. And there's joy!

> Practicing God's presence isn't about perfectionism, and it's not about a product. It's about a process of drawing nearer to a person who loves us and wants us to come close to him, to look to him in every circumstance of life as the eternal source of all goodness and truth."
>
> —KEN BOA[13]

---

* I did not come up with this song and dance on my own. I learned it from Chynna Phillips. Search the internet for "Holy Spirit Activate Steve Harvey," and a video of Chynna on *Family Feud* will explain everything. I hope this video changes your life like it did mine.

Living with Intentionality

I believe practicing the presence of God is vital for us in this day and age because we have so fully divorced the natural and the spiritual. We have forgotten that God woke us up today to do His will on earth, and everything we do—truly everything!—can be done to glorify Him.

So whether you eat or drink, or whatever you do, do everything for the glory of God (1 Corinthians 10:31, NET).

We must live in the temporal in light of the eternal. We must live the here and now in light of our Kingdom calling. This is not multitasking or habit-stacking, this is living our God-given, ordinary life with greater intentionality and purpose. This is what takes an ordinary life and makes it extraordinary. God is the farthest thing from boring or bland. If our lives feel boring and bland to us, we don't need to make a radical change—switch careers, move to Italy, buy a new house, run a marathon—we need to tap into the never-ceasing presence and love of God and ask him to fill our ordinary routines with His extraordinary power and purpose.

Not too long ago, I realized I was having a lot of pretend conversations in my head. You know the kind. It's when you're in the shower, putting on makeup, driving, or doing some other mundane task where your mind wanders and you began rehearsing a conversation you think you'll have in real life with a certain person—maybe it's your boss, a roommate who's gotten on your last nerve, a friend who's disappointed you, or just someone you'd like to give a piece of your mind. I was hosting these imaginary conversations in between my ears at an alarming rate when it dawned on me: *What am I doing?* I was wasting so much mental and emotional energy for absolutely no payoff. Even if I ever had a similar, real-life conversation someday, I was never going to remember all the things I had rehearsed. But more importantly, I realized this was such a waste of time when I could be doing something powerfully productive. I could be praying! I could be talking to God about the situation instead of imagining another person, and actually ask for His help, His guidance, His wisdom, His work. I could pray for the other person. I could ask God to work on their behalf and give them wisdom and guidance. I could ask Him to help me forgive them and love them well. I could ask for His eyes to see them as He does.

That is practicing the presence of God. I didn't do that on my own strength. God, in His kindness, interrupted my stream of consciousness and invited me to leave my imaginary world and enter His presence. He transformed my habit of imaginary conversations into another moment to connect with Him and ask for His guidance. I still find myself having imaginary conversations, but I am becoming quicker in hearing and responding to His invitation to stop and come to Him.

Seed Habits

Practicing the presence of God may seem a bit different than other habits we touch on in this book, but in some ways it is the culmination of all the other habits. Sip by sip, seed by seed, we take in or replant ourselves in God's presence.

If this is a habit you want to cultivate, here are a few ideas to get you started:

- At the end of your day (see note), ask yourself: "Where did I see God present today? When was I aware of His presence? Where did I need God's presence but my eyes were closed?"

- ♦ Note: What is something you always do at the end of the day? (Brush your teeth, take off your makeup, start the dishwasher) Attach it to that. Ideally choose something that takes more than a few seconds so you have time to reflect on your answer.

- In the morning or at night (again, attach this to an existing habit) pray, "Lord, open my eyes to you. Grow my awareness of your presence. Help me to abide in You."
- If falling asleep is regularly a challenge for you, use that time to practice the presence of God!
- Consider choosing one to three existing habits in your life (where your hands are busy but your mind is free) that you can pair with practicing the presence of God.

  - ♦ Doing the dishes or unloading the dishwasher
  - ♦ On your morning walk
  - ♦ Whenever you let out the dog
  - ♦ Folding laundry
  - ♦ Wiping down the counters
  - ♦ Making the bed
  - ♦ Taking a shower
  - ♦ Sweeping* or vacuuming
  - ♦ Preparing ingredients for dinner
  - ♦ Standing in line or waiting in a drive-through

---

* I love to sweep and often tease that my heavenly job will be sweeping the streets of gold. I don't think there's a better way for me to spend my earthly time sweeping than by simultaneously practicing the presence of God!

- Write the word ABIDE or DWELL somewhere in every room of your house or on your phone's lock screen. When you see that word, remember to reconnect with the Lord. You could just quickly pray, "Lord, help me abide."
- Choose a verse below to meditate on or memorize to aid you in your practice:

  - "And He said, 'My presence shall go with you, and I will give you rest'" (Exodus 33:14, NASB).
  - "Search for the LORD and for his strength; continually seek him" (1 Chronicles 16:11).
  - "I know the LORD is always with me. I will not be shaken, for he is right beside me" (Psalm 16:8).
  - "One thing I have asked from the LORD, that I shall seek: That I may dwell in the house of the LORD all the days of my life, to behold the beauty of the LORD and to meditate in His temple" (Psalm 27:4).
  - "Be still, and know that I am God!" (Psalm 46:10).
  - "Happy are those who hear the joyful call to worship, for they will walk in the light of your presence, LORD" (Psalm 89:15).
  - "You will show me the path of life; In Your presence is fullness of joy; At Your right hand are pleasures forevermore" (Psalm 16:11, NKJV).
  - "You will keep in perfect peace all who trust in you, all whose thoughts are fixed on you!" (Isaiah 26:3).
  - "For the LORD your God is living among you. He is a mighty savior. He will take delight in you with gladness. With his love, he will calm all your fears. He

will rejoice over you with joyful songs" (Zephaniah
3:17).

♦   "... we are taking every thought captive to the
obedience of Christ" (2 Corinthians 10:5b, NASB).

♦   "Draw near to God and He will draw near to you"
(James 4:8a, ESV).

♦   "I am the vine, you are the branches; he who abides
in Me and I in him, he bears much fruit, for apart
from Me you can do nothing" (John 15:5, NASB
1995).

Chapter Review

• Practicing the presence of God is simply developing a
continual awareness of God's presence throughout
your day.

• The outcome of this practice is not somber or serious,
but rather JOY—there is fullness of joy in the presence of
God.[14]

• Jesus taught His followers that the key to a fruitful, spiritual life is by abiding in Him and His love.

• Practicing the presence of God is learning to abide in Him
continually.

• All other habits we've discussed in this book also usher us
into practicing the presence of God.

• The best place to start this habit is by asking God to help
you abide in Him. This prayer is undoubtedly His will
for you, so you can have confidence He will give you what
you ask.

Homework

- Flip back to chapter two and prayerfully review your existing habits you wrote down. Are there two or three habits you could attach to practicing the presence of God? Write a Seed Habit formula or two to try out this practice.

After I **open the dishwasher to load it**, I will **practice the presence of God (or abide in Him)** by **praying a quick prayer*** and **imagining Him with me**.

After I **begin to feel overwhelmed by my circumstances**, I will **sing "Holy Spirit activate!" at the top of my lungs**.

- Reflect: Do you know someone who seems to practice this habit well? If so, make it your mission to connect with them this week to share what you're learning and ask for their insight.

---

* Write out your quick prayer. Here's an example to get you going: *Lord, I am here. You are always with me. Open my eyes to Your presence. Fill me with Your* [joy, peace, love, whatever you need from Him in that moment].

CHAPTER NINE

Scattering Seeds

"The Kingdom of God is like a farmer who scatters seed on the ground. Night and day, while he's asleep or awake, the seed sprouts and grows, but he does not understand how it happens."

—MARK 4:26–27

THE FARMER MAY PLANT THE SEEDS, BUT HE DOESN'T CAUSE THE growth. He scatters them on the ground, and they grow at all hours of the day—no matter if he's milking a cow, balancing his budget, having a difficult conversation with his spouse, or sleeping at the end of a long day. In the same way, you and I may scatter dozens of Seed Habits throughout our days, but it is only the Lord who causes growth in our lives. Practicing spiritual habits is a choice we make that puts us in a posture that allows God to transform us. It's a choice we make to show up and be the person God created us to be in the soil where He has planted us.

Spiritual Habits aren't activities for us to achieve or measure our spiritual maturity. They don't earn God's love or curry His favor. But they do tether us to Him. They help us know and love God more deeply and sustain fellowship with Him, and shape us to reflect His character. They put us on the path to who we will ultimately become. *Who do you want to become?*

Throughout this book I have given you dozens of ways to create Seed Habits—small, easy spiritual habits that fit into your day. These are not ways to hack the spiritual life. They are simply small steps to help you begin creating habits that will take deep roots in your life if you will only begin with a little bit of intention. If you will only plant a few tiny seeds.

In Mark 4, Jesus is recorded telling three back-to-back stories about seeds. The first is the longest—and one you're probably familiar with— about seeds that fell into four different environments and yielded varying results. The second story is just two verses that I included at the beginning of this chapter. The third and final seed story is also one you've likely heard—the parable of the mustard seed.

> Jesus said, "How can I describe the Kingdom of God? What story should I use to illustrate it? It is like a mustard seed planted in the ground. It is the smallest of all seeds, but it becomes the largest of all garden plants; it grows long branches, and birds can make nests in its shade" (Mark 4:30–32).

The mustard seed is tiny—roughly one to two millimeters in diameter—which is about the size of the tip of a ballpoint pen. They are smooth, round spheres that come in a variety of colors. And they can grow into a shrub or small tree that is over six to ten feet tall with broad, green leaves and clusters of vibrant, yellow flowers. Jesus's point is that the Kingdom of God may start very small, barely even noticeable, but it yields mighty results because it's His work.

T he example of the mustard seed should prevent us from judging the significance of results by the size of the beginnings."

—D. E. NINEHAM[1]

We see this dozens of times in scripture. God loves to use the small, weak, insignificant things of this world to illuminate His glory. God loves the underdog, and God loves even the smallest of beginnings. He loves your Seed Habits because they are your humble ways of saying, "Lord, I want to grow spiritually. I want to be more connected to you. I want to love you more deeply and pour out your love more often to others." He will take that humble, small beginning and fuel it with his power to take that mustard seed of a habit and grow it into something far beyond what you could imagine.

By the end of this book, you may have created and implemented several Seed Habits that have truly begun to stick. You may even be experiencing growth with one or two of them. Praise God! I am confident that if you want to scatter spiritual habits throughout your day and identify a way you will do it, God will bless you in your efforts and desires. I also know that you are human, and just like me, you are going to be knocked off your normal routine and look back after a day or a week and realize some or all of those Seed Habits you worked so hard at planting into your everyday life fell to the wayside. This is when we can remind ourselves that although we scatter the seeds, He causes growth, and we can make a choice to get back to our small, easy habits that fit into our day. Remember, it only takes flossing one tooth to keep the habit of flossing alive. It only takes one verse to keep the habit of Bible reading alive. It only takes one minute of solitude to keep the habit of being alone with God alive.

When we cultivate the habit of showing up, we are voting over and over for the person we want to become.[2] We begin with small and easy Seed Habits that fit into our day—not because we can't do hard things or we don't have enough discipline to "go big," but because it's the proven way to create habits that will infiltrate our ordinary days and add up to a lifetime of faithfully following Jesus. When God told Zechariah to lead the rebuilding of the Temple, He warned him not to despise small beginnings. On the contrary, He said, God rejoices to see the work begin (Zechariah 4:10)!

Each Seed Habit you create, God rejoices over! Each moment you choose to reconnect to Him, He delights in it. Each time you change your focus from your physical circumstance to an eternal perspective, He celebrates.

Practicing spiritual habits should be life-giving, not draining. It should increase your joy, not make you cranky. It should stir up in you more compassion and love for others, not make you judgmental. These habits are meant to draw you closer to God, shaping you to reflect His character—making you more loving, joyful, peaceful, patient, kind, and faithful.

If a habit is leaving you drained or weary, it's an opportunity to pause and recalibrate. Spiritual habits are not about striving in your own strength or earning God's favor; they are about abiding in Him. And abiding in Him through devouring the Bible, being devoted to prayer, seeking solitude with Him, celebrating and being thankful, pursuing Christ-centered friendships, and practicing the presence of God all lead to greater joy.

So, I will ask you the question we began with one more time: Who do you want to become, and what small, spiritual habits can you start to help you get there?

When you imagine yourself at ninety years old, who are you? Are you on the path to becoming her? Your spiritual habits, the automatic ways you have cultivated to connect with God, will accumulate day after day, resulting in a woman who is tethered to Jesus and filled with more joy, hope, and love than you can possibly fathom.

May the God of all joy fill your Seed Habits with His resurrection power.

May He do in you, and through your humble efforts, what only He can do.

May He grow in you a deeper love, joy, and peace that the world will gaze at in wonder.

And may He make your ordinary days add up to an extraordinary life tethered to Him.

APPENDIX A

Spiritual Health Check:
A No-Judgment Self-Assessment

In this season of life, I am more often . . .

❑ Energized   ❑ Exhausted

❑ Joyful   ❑ Bitter

❑ Peaceful   ❑ Anxious

❑ Quick to forgive   ❑ Quick to anger or hurt

❑ Gentle   ❑ Harsh

❑ Warm to others   ❑ Cold to others

❑ Able to control myself   ❑ Quick to lose control

When was the last time I read my Bible in a way that actually impacted me or my day?

❑ Today   ❑ Within the last week

❑ Within the last month   ❑ It's been several months

❑ It's been a long time

When was the last time I prayed in such a way that made me feel connected to God, deepened my trust in Him, and gave me greater peace and joy about my circumstances?

❑ Today   ❑ Within the last week

❑ Within the last month   ❑ It's been several months

❑ It's been a long time

When was the last time I was aware of God's presence with me in an ordinary moment of my day?

❑ Today   ❑ Within the last week

❑ Within the last month   ❑ It's been several months

❑ It's been a long time

When was the last time I took a moment to be grateful for or celebrate things God has done in my life?

❑ Today   ❑ Within the last week

❑ Within the last month   ❑ It's been several months

❑ It's been a long time

When was the last time I had a moment of solitude when I felt connected to God in a way that refreshed me?

❑ Today   ❑ Within the last week

❑ Within the last month   ❑ It's been several months

❑ It's been a long time

When was the last time I connected with a friend or family member in a way that pointed me to Christ, reminded me of His goodness, or allowed me to love and encourage them?

❑ Today   ❑ Within the last week

❑ Within the last month   ❑ It's been several months

❑ It's been a long time

Overall, I am _____ when it comes to my spiritual health.

❑ Happy   ❑ Content

❑ Restless   ❑ Disappointed

How do you feel? Remember, no judgment (from me or you!). You are not allowed to be mad at yourself if you don't love your answers. God is not mad at you. He loves you. He sees you. He is intimately aware of all that is going on with you, and He is inviting you into a deeper walk with Him. He wants to empower you, energize you, and make you illuminate with love, joy, and peace. He wants to slowly transform you into a ninety-year-old woman who radiates like a star in the dark night sky.[1]

It would be easy to feel overwhelmed, like you need to read this entire book and begin tackling every spiritual discipline we discuss. Hear me say loud and clear: Please do not do that. Read the whole book to get a lay of the land and then pick one discipline you want to start with, or jump straight to the chapter you know you need. Don't let everything become the enemy of something. Remember: one tiny habit, one tiny seed. Make it small, make it easy, make it fit, and let it grow.

APPENDIX B

How to Study the Bible

"The basic difference between Bible reading and Bible study is simply a pen and paper."[1]

STUDYING THE BIBLE IS A LIFELONG LEARNING PROCESS. CHARLES Spurgeon famously wrote, "Nobody ever outgrows scripture; the book widens and deepens with our years."[2] It can be easy to become overwhelmed with the vast number of Bible study methods, techniques, and resources, but don't let that stop you from starting small and easy. Our goal in studying the Bible is simply to wade in deeper waters little by little. You don't need to go from dipping your toes in the water to deep-sea diving. Just take one small step at a time. Here are a few tips to get you started.

Observe

After reading a passage of scripture a few times—maybe in a different English translation—grab a pen and jot down some things you notice in the text. Here are some observation questions to consider:

- Note the five W's and H—Who, What, When, Where, Why, and How? Ask: Who was involved? What happened? When did it occur? Where did it take place and why? How did it come about?
- What words or concepts are repeated?
- Are there any contrasts or comparisons?
- Are there any lists?
- Are there any cause-and-effect relationships?
- Is there a command, promise, or warning?
- Are there any unusual or surprising details?
- Write down any questions you have about the text or note things you don't understand.

Interpretation

- What is the author trying to say here? What is the point? Summarize what you read in a sentence.
- What does this passage teach me about God, Jesus, and/or the Holy Spirit?
- What does this passage teach me about mankind?
- What did this mean to the original audience?
- This is the point where you utilize commentaries and other resources to help you understand the historical context, original language, and other insights.

Apply

- How does this passage apply to my life?
- Is there a promise, command, or warning I need to pay attention to?

- What is one small, easy way I can put this scripture into practice today?
- Ask Martin Luther's three questions:

    - In light of this passage, how can we praise God?
    - In light of this passage, what do we need to confess?
    - In light of this passage, what do we need to ask God for?

Additional Resources

When you're reading to go deeper, here are a few resources I recommend.

BibleProject: Whenever you study a book of the Bible, I highly recommend heading to the BibleProject website and watching their video summary of the book.

Tom Constable's Notes: Another free online resource. Dr. Constable has written a verse-by-verse commentary on every book of the Bible. He offers a variety of interpretations of difficult passages and includes quotes from hundreds of other commentaries.

Living By the Book by Howard Hendricks: Professor Hendricks has written a book and workbook that gives you a step-by-step approach to inductive Bible study.

Women of the Word by Jen Wilkin: This is an inviting, easy read that gives you both the big picture and a "how to" overview on studying the Bible.

APPENDIX C

Small Group Questions

Chapter One
The Practice of Spiritual Habits

Who did you think of as your "favorite elderly woman" at the beginning of the chapter?

What has been your background or experience with spiritual disciplines?

Did anything from this chapter challenge your perspective on spiritual disciplines?

What did you think about Dallas Willard's golden triangle of spiritual formation?

What spiritual habit are you most excited to dive into and why?

What was your biggest takeaway from this chapter?

Who do you want to be in the last decade of your life, and are you taking baby steps toward becoming her? What needs to change?

Chapter Two
So Long, "Go Big or Go Home"

How has the "go big or go home" mentality impacted you personally? How have you seen it play out when you approach spiritual habits?

When you consider your current spiritual habits, are they putting you on the path to being the person you want to become?

In this chapter, you read about how an airplane from Los Angeles to New York City can be taken off route and will land in Washington, DC, (225 miles off destination) if the pilot adjusts the heading only by 3.5 degrees. Have you seen this play out in your personal life?

What was your initial response to the framework of make it small, make it easy, make it fit, let it grow?

Did you encounter anything in this chapter that changed your perspective or brought something new to light?

What did you like most or find the most challenging in this chapter?

Chapter Three
Devour the Bible

This chapter covered five ways we can devour the Bible: reading, studying, hearing, meditating, and memorizing. Which of these are most familiar to you, and which ones feel like more of a challenge?

Sometimes we read the Bible out of obligation, to gain information, or to seek transformation. How have you seen those different approaches play out in your own life?

What has helped you build a sticky, life-giving habit of engaging with scripture?

Did you try any Seed Habits related to Bible intake this week? What worked well for you, and what didn't?

What was your biggest takeaway from this chapter? Were there any lines or ideas that really stuck with you?

Chapter Four
Devoted to Prayer

What's one area of your life you wish you prayed about more regularly?

How would you describe your prayer life in this current season—devoted, watchful, without ceasing, dry, stagnant, boring, growing, or something else?

Was there anything in this chapter that shifted your perspective on prayer or stood out in a new way?

How have so-called unanswered prayers impacted your prayer life or your faith journey?

Did you try any Seed Habits related to prayer this week? What worked well and what didn't?

What was your biggest takeaway from this chapter? Any highlights or moments that really stuck with you?

Chapter Five
Seeking Solitude

What has your past experience with solitude been like— life-giving, challenging, or unfamiliar?

After reading this chapter, does solitude feel like a spiritual habit that could benefit you in this season of life? Why or why not?

What might biblical solitude look like for you personally in the rhythm of your everyday life?

This chapter suggested that our phones are often the biggest enemy of solitude, pulling our attention away from heavenly things. Do you agree or disagree? Were you prompted to make any changes?

Did you try any Seed Habits related to solitude this week? What worked well and what didn't?

What was your biggest takeaway from this chapter? Were there any moments, phrases, or ideas that really stuck with you?

*Close out your group time with a minute (or five!) of solitude and silence.

Chapter Six
Toasting to Joy!

How would you describe your relationship with joy in this current season? Are you chasing it, missing it, or living fully in it?

Have you ever experienced something that felt like a true biblical celebration—like a wedding, a celebration of life, or something else? What made it feel like a celebration unto the Lord?

What's one thing you can genuinely celebrate right now, no matter how big or small?

What does it look like to practice thanksgiving in the midst of hardship or disappointment?

Did you try any Seed Habits related to celebration or gratitude this week? What worked well for you, and what didn't?

What was your biggest takeaway from this chapter? Were there any phrases, moments, or ideas that really stuck with you?

Chapter Seven
Cultivating Friendship

Would you say you're currently content, dissatisfied, or thriving when it comes to friendship? Why?

Can you think of a time when a friend went out of their way to show up for you during a hard season? What did that mean to you?

Philippians 2 calls us to consider others above ourselves. What might that look like practically in friendship?

Why do you think vulnerability is so hard—and where have you seen it lead to meaningful growth or connection?

If someone described you as a friend, what do you hope they'd say? What kind of friend do you want to be known as?

Did you implement any Seed Habits in this area this week? Share what worked and what didn't.

What was your biggest takeaway from this chapter? (Any highlights you made?)

Chapter Eight
Abiding in Him
(Practicing the Presence of God)

How aware are you of God's presence in your everyday life? Are there particular moments or places where you are more aware? Was this spiritual habit a new idea for you?

This chapter explored the idea of finding God in ordinary, everyday moments. What's one "ordinary" part of your day that could become sacred if you were intentionally aware of God's presence in it?

What gets in the way of your ability to notice or enjoy God's nearness? (Think: distractions, pace of life, noise, internal pressure, etc.)

Was there anything in this chapter that shifted your perspective on living your ordinary day with an eternal perspective?

Did you try any Seed Habits related to practicing God's presence this week? What worked well and what didn't?

What was your biggest takeaway from this chapter? Were there any phrases, verses, or ideas that really stuck with you?

Chapter Nine
Scattering Seeds

Looking back over all the chapters, which spiritual habit impacted you the most—and why?

Was there a specific Seed Habit you implemented that stuck with you or surprised you in its effectiveness?

How has your perspective on spiritual growth changed since reading this book?

Which chapter or concept challenged you the most? What did that reveal about your current season or rhythms?

What would it look like for you to take the next faithful step in your everyday walk with Jesus after finishing this book?

If you were to recommend this book to a friend, what would you tell them it's about?

ACKNOWLEDGMENTS

THIS BOOK STANDS ON THE SHOULDERS OF GODLY MEN AND WOMEN who have devoted their lives to strengthening the church through their writings on spiritual formation. Influential voices like Richard Foster, Dallas Willard, John Ortberg, Ken Boa, Ruth Haley Barton, Adele Ahlberg Calhoun, and many others have profoundly impacted my life and largely shaped the content of this book. I am deeply grateful for their labors and ministries.

I am also immensely thankful for James Clear, BJ Fogg, and Charles Duhigg, whose work on the science of habit formation opened my eyes to how our daily habits truly dictate the outcomes of our lives. Without *Atomic Habits* by James Clear and *The Celebration of Discipline* by Richard Foster, this book would not exist.

My deepest gratitude belongs to my parents, Michael and Cindy Easley, who have modeled a life marked by spiritual habits in a way that permanently shaped my own soul. To my dad, who handed me a copy of Richard Foster's book when I was in high school and who instilled in me a deep love for God's Word. And to my mom, who I found every morning curled up on the couch with her coffee and Bible, who showed me how to be the woman God created me to be in the everyday moments of life—thank you. To you both, your faithful prayers continue to echo in my life. Your examples are living testimonies of what it looks like to walk closely with God.

Carly Kellerman, my agent extraordinaire—what a dream it is to work with you. I still can't believe you picked me. I felt like the tired kid who assumed she'd be chosen last in dodgeball—but then the sharp, confident, and cool captain (you) pointed at me and said, "You! Let's go!" I'll never forget what it meant to feel at my lowest and know you believed I had something to offer. I'm so thankful we get to do this together.

I'm also incredibly thankful for Beth Adams, my wise and thoughtful editor. Thank you for believing this book was important and needed! And thank you for your gentle guidance throughout the entire process and making this book way better than I could have on my own. Also vital to this entire process is the Worthy Team: Daisy Hutton, Hailey Juen, Marissa Arrigoni, Cat Hoort, Katie Robison, Taylor Peterson, Ella Rose Murphy, Faith Fiorile, and Fred Francis. Thank you for all that you do behind the scenes to make this book a reality. I'm so grateful for each of you.

A special shoutout to the Tier Moms (Kelly, Kristen, and Kiersten) for letting me use you as sounding boards as I began to flesh out this book concept. And to the 2,100+ women who took my online survey! Talk about a mustard seed story! Your participation in that survey ultimately led to the very book you hold in your hands.

A million hugs to my three extraordinary kids. Thank you for giving up Tuesday nights and Fridays with me so I could focus on this book. Thank you for always being excited to celebrate the various milestones of this journey. What a joy it is to be your mom.

And to my insanely supportive and encouraging husband, Tyler— I'm so glad you're my person. This book would not exist without your never-ending support, and I certainly wouldn't be who I am without you. If there were a Proverbs 32 man, you'd be it.

Finally, if you're reading this—thank you! A book is nothing without readers. I am so grateful you have allowed me to spend this time with you. I have prayed for every single one of you who picked up this book—that God would meet you right where you are and that you would be equipped to do the good work He has called you to do.

To the goodness and glory of God!

NOTES

Introduction

1. This is one of the frequent phrases that John Wimber, founder of the Vineyard Church Movement, used to say. You can read all about Wimber's life and his other highly quotable phrases in a book aptly titled *Never Trust a Leader Without a Limp* by Glenn Schroder.

Chapter One

1. Dr. Howard Taylor and Mrs. Howard Taylor, *Hudson Taylor's Spiritual Secret* (Moody Publishers, 1989), 17.

2. Jen Wilkin, *Women of the Word: How to Study the Bible with Both Our Hearts and Our Minds* (Crossway, 2014).

3. Dallas Willard, "Looking Like Jesus," *Christianity Today*, August 20, 1990; reprinted in *The Great Omission* (HarperCollins, 2006); also available at: https://dwillard.org/resources/articles/looking-like-jesus-divine-resources-for-a-changed-life-are-always-available.

4. Richard Foster, *Celebration of Discipline: The Path to Spiritual Growth* (HarperOne, 2018), xiv.

5. Foster, *Celebration of Discipline*, xv.

6. Foster, *Celebration of Discipline*, xvi.

7. *Faith in Practice: A Biblical Study of Spiritual Disciplines*, She Reads Truth, accessed November 4, 2024, https://shereadstruth.com/plans/faith-in-practice-a-biblical-study-of-spiritual-disciplines/.

8. "Spiritual Disciplines," Renovaré, https://renovare.org/about/ideas/spiritual-disciplines.

9. Donald S. Whitney, *Spiritual Disciplines for the Christian Life* (NavPress, 1991), 4.

10. Whitney, *Spiritual Disciplines*, 13.

11. John Ortberg, *The Life You've Always Wanted: Spiritual Disciplines for Ordinary People* (Zondervan, 1997), 43.

12. Beth Moore, *Chasing Vines: Finding Your Way to an Immensely Fruitful Life* (Tyndale, 2020).

13. Gary M. Burge, *The NIV Application Commentary: John* (Zondervan, 2000), 416.

14. Moore, *Chasing Vines*, 103.

15. Jamie Goode, "Struggling Vines Produce Better Wines," Wineanorak, http://www.wineanorak.com/struggle.htm.

16. Foster, *Celebration of Discipline*, 2.

17. Moore, *Chasing Vines*, 79.

18. Moore, *Chasing Vines*, 79–80.

19. Justin Irving, *LD102 The Ministry Leader and the Inner Life*, Logos Mobile Education (Lexham Press, 2016).

Chapter Two

1. Zechariah 4:10, NLT.

2. James Clear, *Atomic Habits: Tiny Changes, Remarkable Results: An Easy & Proven Way to Build Good Habits & Break Bad Ones* (Avery, 2018).

3. Annie Dillard, *The Writing Life* (Picador, 1990), 32.

4. Clear, *Atomic Habits*, 34.

5. Clear, *Atomic Habits*, 6.

6. Clear, *Atomic Habits*, 163.

7. Clear, *Atomic Habits*, 15.

8. Dolly Parton, "9 to 5," track 1 on *9 to 5* and *Odd Jobs*, RCA Victor, 1980, LP.

9. BJ Fogg, *Tiny Habits: The Small Changes That Change Everything* (Houghton Mifflin Harcourt, 2020), 4.

10. Fogg, *Tiny Habits*, 150.

Chapter Three

1. Augustine, *On Christian Doctrine*, trans. D. W. Robertson Jr. (Bobbs-Merrill, 1958), 2.6.

2. "Graham's Secret to Staying Connected to God," The Wesleyan Church, accessed November 8, 2024, https://www.wesleyan.org/grahams-secret-staying-connected-god.

3. Arnold Cole and Pamela Caudill Ovwigho, "Understanding the Bible Engagement Challenge: Scientific Evidence for the Power of 4," Center for Bible Engagement, December 2009, https://bttbfiles.com/web/docs/cbe/Scientific_Evidence_for_the_Power_of_4.pdf.

4. John Mark Comer, *Practicing the Way: Be with Jesus. Become like Him. Do as He Did* (WaterBrook, 2024), 86.

5. "Billy Graham's Love of Scripture Leaves Lasting Impression on His Grandson," BillyGraham.org, accessed November 8, 2024, https://web.archive.org /web/20241105065504/https://billygraham.org/story/billy-grahams-love-of-scripture -leaves-lasting-impression-on-his-grandson/.

6. Robert J. Morgan, *100 Bible Verses Everyone Should Know by Heart* (B&H Publishing Group, 2010), 39.

7. Howard Hendricks, *Living by the Book* (Moody Publishers, 1991), 19.

8. John Pollock, *Billy Graham: Evangelist to the World* (Harper & Row, 1979), 248.

9. Whitney, *Spiritual Disciplines*, 22.

10. "The Tremendous Value of Listening to God's Word Read Aloud," ESV .org, accessed April 8, 2025, https://www.esv.org/articles/the-tremendous-value-of -listening-to-gods-word-read-aloud-for-esv-org/.

11. John Pollock, *Billy Graham: The Authorized Biography* (Bethany House Publishers, 2004), 248.

12. Glenna Marshall, *Memorizing Scripture* (Crossway, 2023), 10.

13. Morgan, *100 Bible Verses*, 4.

14. Morgan, *100 Bible Verses*, 39.

15. Marshall, *Memorizing Scripture*, 1.

16. Morgan, *100 Bible Verses*, 11.

Chapter Four

1. R. J. Foster, *Celebration of Discipline*, Special Anniversary Edition (HarperOne, 2018), 33.

2. The quote "When I pray, coincidences happen; when I don't, they don't" is attributed to Archbishop William Temple, who served as the Archbishop of Canterbury from 1942 to 1944. The earliest documented source of this quote appears in David Watson's book *Called & Committed: World-Changing Discipleship*, which was published in 1982. While this attribution is widely accepted, it's important to note that the quote's precise origin remains somewhat uncertain.

3. Wayne A. Grudem, *Systematic Theology: An Introduction to Biblical Doctrine* (Inter-Varsity Press; Zondervan Publishing House, 2004), 628.

4. BibleProject, "The Lord's Prayer," video, 5:45, accessed January 8, 2025, https: //bibleproject.com/explore/video/lords-prayer/.

5. Søren Kierkegaard, *Provocations: Spiritual Writings of Kierkegaard*, edited by Charles E. Moore (Plough Publishing House, 2007), 349.

6. Paige Brown, *Singled Out for Him: A Biblical View of Singleness* (Park Cities Presbyterian Church, n.d.), https://static.pcpc.org/articles/singles/singledout.pdf.

7. Kierkegaard, *Provocations*, 347.

8. Dallas Willard, *The Spirit of the Disciplines: Understanding How God Changes Lives* (HarperSanFrancisco, 1991), 184.

9. Foster, *Celebration of Discipline*, 33.

10. Foster, *Celebration of Discipline*, 35.

11. Karl Barth, *Prayer: According to the Catechisms of the Reformation*, Stenographic Records of Three Seminars, trans. Sara F. Terrien (The Westminster Press, 1946), 23

12. Willard, *The Spirit of the Disciplines*, 186.

Chapter Five

1. Foster, *Celebration of Discipline*, 98.

2. Matthew 14:13.

3. Matthew 14:23.

4. Mark 1:35, Luke 4:42.

5. Kenneth Boa, *Life in the Presence of God: Practices for Living in Light of Eternity* (InterVarsity Press, 2017), 59, Kindle.

6. Matthew 4:1–11.

7. Luke 6:12.

8. Matthew 26:36.

9. Comer, *Practicing the Way*, 183.

10. Henri Nouwen, *The Spiritual Life: Eight Essential Titles by Henri Nouwen* (HarperOne, 2016), 24.

11. Dianne Whiting, "Solitude," in *Evangelical Dictionary of Christian Education*, ed. Michael J. Anthony et al., Baker Reference Library (Baker Academic, 2001), 651.

12. Adele Ahlberg Calhoun, *Spiritual Disciplines Handbook* (InterVarsity Press, 2015), x.

13. Cal Newport, *Digital Minimalism* (Portfolio, 2019), 101.

14. Trevor Wheelwright, "Cell Phone Usage Stats 2025: Americans Check Their Phones 205 Times a Day," January 1, 2025, https://www.reviews.org/mobile/cell-phone-addiction/.

15. Josh Howarth, "Time Spent Using Smartphones (2024 Statistics)," June 4, 2024, https://web.archive.org/web/20250112153505/https://explodingtopics.com/blog/smartphone-usage-stats.

16. Ortberg, *The Life You've Always Wanted*, 82.

17. Colossians 3:2.

18. John Mark Comer, *The Ruthless Elimination of Hurry: How to Stay Emotionally Healthy and Spiritually Alive in the Chaos of the Modern World* (WaterBrook, 2019), 54.

19. Mark 6:31, ESV.

20. Whitney, *Spiritual Disciplines*, 244.

Chapter Six

1. Lewis B. Smedes, *How Can It Be All Right When Everything Is All Wrong?* (Harper Collins, 1992), 17.

2. Foster, *Celebration of Discipline*, 191.

3. 2 Samuel 6:21, NASB.

4. Willard, *The Spirit of Disciplines*, 181.

5. Shauna Niequist, *Celebrate Every Day: Seeing the Extraordinary in the Ordinary* (Zondervan, 2024), Kindle edition.

6. Ken Boa, *Conformed to His Image* (Zondervan Academic, 2020), 75.

7. Foster, *Celebration of Discipline*, 96.

8. Ortberg, *The Life You've Always Wanted*, 61.

9. Willard, *The Spirit of Disciplines*, 179.

10. Philippians 4:6–7, NLT.

11. Nicholas Kerry, Ria Chhabra, and Jeremy D. W. Clifton, "Being Thankful for What You Have: A Systematic Review of Evidence for the Effect of Gratitude on Life Satisfaction," *Psychology Research and Behavior Management* 16 (2023): 4799–4816, https://www.dovepress.com/article/download/88518.

12. Alex M. Wood, Jeffrey J. Froh, and Adam W. A. Geraghty, "Gratitude and Well-Being: A Review and Theoretical Integration," *Clinical Psychology Review* 30, no. 7 (2010): 890–905, doi:10.1016/j.cpr.2010.03.005.

13. Kerry A. Kinney, Shania M. Clifford, Devon C. Cole, and Robert A. Emmons, "Being Thankful for What You Have: A Longitudinal Investigation of Gratitude and Well-Being," *Psychology Research and Behavior Management* 17 (2024): 1137–1149, https://doi.org/10.2147/PRBM.S385932.

14. Michael E. Mccullough, Robert A. Emmons, and Jo-Ann Tsang, "The Grateful Disposition: A Conceptual and Empirical Topography," *Journal of Personal and Social Psychology* 82, no.1 (2002): 112–127, doi:10.1037/0022-3514.82.1.112.

15. Wenceslao Unanue et al., "The Reciprocal Relationship Between Gratitude and Life Satisfaction: Evidence from Two Longitudinal Field Studies," *Personality and Social Psychology* 10 (2019), https://www.frontiersin.org/journals/psychology/articles/10.3389/fpsyg.2019.02480/full.

Chapter Seven

1. Drew Hunter, *Made for Friendship: The Relationship That Halves Our Sorrows and Doubles Our Joys* (Crossway, 2018), 23, Kindle edition.

2. "Daily Loneliness Afflicts One in Five in U.S.," *Gallup News*, last modified December 7, 2023, https://news.gallup.com/poll/651881/daily-loneliness-afflicts-one-five.aspx.

3. American Psychiatric Association, "New APA Poll: One in Three Americans Feels Lonely Every Week," *APA Newsroom*, May 2, 2023, https://psychiatry.org/news-room/news-releases/new-apa-poll-one-in-three-americans-feels-lonely-e.

4. Cara Lynn Shultz, "Former Surgeon General Vivek Murthy Says Loneliness Is a 'Deep Pain' Exacerbated by Social Media," *People*, January 21, 2025, https://people.com/vivek-murthy-loneliness-causes-deep-pain-surgeon-general-rainn-wilson-8777615.

5. Ramsey Solutions, *The State of Mental Health 2022*, RamseySolutions.com, May 1, 2023, https://www.ramseysolutions.com/personal-growth/state-of-mental-health-2022-research.

6. John Delony, *Building a Non-Anxious Life* (Ramsey Press, 2023), 115.

7. Hunter, *Made for Friendship*, 28.

8. Genesis 1:26.

9. J. C. Ryle, "The Best Friend," *Grace Gems*, accessed April 15, 2025, https://gracegems.org/Ryle/best_friend.htm.

10. Hunter, *Made for Friendship*.

11. Philippians 2:3–4.

12. Philippians 2:4, NASB.

Chapter Eight

1. Charles R. Swindoll, *Bedside Blessings: 365 Days of Inspirational Thoughts* (Thomas Nelson, 2011), 167.

2. Brother Lawrence, *The Practice of the Presence of God in Modern English* (Independently Published, 2013), Kindle edition.

3. Lawrence, *The Practice of the Presence of God*, 22.

4. Mark Galli and Ted Olsen, "Introduction," *131 Christians Everyone Should Know* (Broadman & Holman Publishers, 2000), 273.

5. Lawrence, *The Practice of the Presence of God*, 22.

6. Lawrence, *The Practice of the Presence of God*, 24.

7. John 15:11.

8. C. S. Lewis, *Letters to Malcolm: Chiefly on Prayer* (Harcourt Brace Jovanovich, 1964), 75.

9. Frank C. Laubach, *Letters by a Modern Mystic* (Fleming H. Revell, 1937), 7.

10. Laubach, *Letters by a Modern Mystic*, 7.

11. John 16:23–27.

12. Joseph de Beaufort, *Brother Lawrence: The Practice of the Presence of God the Best Rule of a Holy Life, Being Conversations and Letters of Nicholas Herman of Lorraine (Brother Lawrence)* (F. H. Revell, 1895), 20.

13. Boa, *Life in the Presence of God*, 30, Kindle edition.

14. Psalm 16:11.

Chapter Nine

1. D. E. Nineham, *Saint Mark*, Pelican Gospel Commentary series (Penguin Books, 1963), 144.

2. Clear, *Atomic Habits*, 38.

Appendix A

1. Philippians 2:15.

Appendix B

1. Whitney, *Spiritual Disciplines for the Christian Life*, 32.

2. Charles Haddon Spurgeon, *The Metropolitan Tabernacle Pulpit*, Vol. 17 (Passmore & Alabaster, 1872), 598.

ABOUT THE AUTHOR

Hanna Seymour is an author, Bible teacher, and podcast host who is passionate about encouraging and equipping women to walk faithfully with Christ in their everyday lives. She holds a BA from James Madison University, an M.Ed. in higher education and student affairs from the University of South Carolina, and an MA in biblical studies from Redemption Seminary. As a seminary graduate, wife, and mom of three, she brings a relatable, grace-filled perspective to spiritual growth, especially through small, everyday habits. Hanna also authored *The College Girl's Survival Guide*, which was featured on *Fox & Friends* and *FamilyLife Today*. Whether she's writing, teaching, or recording, Hanna is passionate about making spiritual growth accessible, sustainable, and rooted in the truth of God's Word. Find her at hannaseymour.com.